THE GLORY
OF THE CROSS

THE GLORY
OF THE CROSS

Our Life through His Death

STEVE HANKINS

The Glory of the Cross—
Our Life through His Death

Unless noted otherwise, Scripture quotations are taken from the New American Standard Bible® (NASB), Copyright © 1960, 1962, 1963, 1968, 1971, 1972, 1973, 1975, 1977, 1995 by The Lockman Foundation Used by permission. www.Lockman.org

This Edition: 2021

ISBN: 978-1-7373836-1-1

Design and Typesetting by Great Writing Publications
www.greatwriting.org
Taylors, SC, USA

IS20210618

To

My grandsons and granddaughters

*Ethan, Abby, Shane, Nellie, Adelaide, Elijah,
Ford, Isaiah, Gideon, and Anna*

Proverbs 17:6

Preface

The death of Christ, affirmed in its full significance by His resurrection, is the central truth of Christianity. It is the central event of history. As the Apostle wrote, "But when the fullness of time came, God sent forth His Son, born of a woman, born under the Law, so that He might redeem those who were under the Law, that we might receive the adoption of sons. Because you are sons, God has sent forth the Spirit of His Son into our hearts, crying, "Abba! Father!" (Gal 4:4–6). His birth and subsequent life were all designed for this greatest achievement for mankind—their redemption. This makes it a primary focus of the Christian's interest. Understanding it in all its depth and implications increases the believer's faith, joy, and zealous service for His glory.

That the Word of God is to be the daily meditation of the disciple of Jesus is a truth reiterated often in the Word itself. Its transformative power and daily strengthening, administered to the heart of the follower of Christ by the Holy Spirit, is indispensable to fruitful Christian living. Combining this truth with the centrality of the Cross in Scripture urges a focus on it as a means of growth in the grace and knowledge of the Lord Jesus Christ (2 Pet 3:18). This book, containing thirty-one chapters, provides a month-long path to this goal, ideally to be read monthly in its entirety, as part of a disciple's daily devotional exercises. The chapters are brief, allowing for thorough thought and maximum understanding.

The outcome sought through time spent in the Scriptures about the Cross is that it will be glorified in the heart of the believer and before all those he knows, as the title of this work reflects. For the Cross to be glorified means it will be thought of rightly, in all its eternal magnificence and importance, by all who learn of it. Through this, its drawing power on the hearts of men will occur and they will trust what Jesus did for them through His death and resurrection.

For the believer, the Cross of Jesus becomes a daily motivation to a life of self-denial, willing sacrificial service, and faith-filled obedience. Luke 9:23 becomes the great directive of his life: "If anyone wishes to come after Me, he must deny himself, and take up his cross daily and follow me." It is my prayer that this will become the life of every reader of this book.

Steve Hankins
Greenville, South Carolina
June 21, 2021

Key Texts on the Cross

And Jesus answered them, saying, "The hour has come for the Son of Man to be glorified. Truly, truly, I say to you, unless a grain of wheat falls into the earth and dies, it remains alone; but if it dies, it bears much fruit.
John 12:23–24

"And He was saying to them all, 'If anyone wishes to come after Me, he must deny himself, and take up his cross daily, and follow me."
Luke 9:23

"I have been crucified with Christ; and it is no longer I who live, but Christ lives in me; and the life which I now live in the flesh I live by faith in the Son of God, who loved me and gave Himself up for me."
Galatians 2:20

"But may it never be that I would boast, except in the cross of our Lord Jesus Christ, through which the world has been crucified to me, and I to the world."
Galatians 6:14

"For I determined to know nothing among you except Jesus Christ, and Him crucified."
1 Corinthians 2:2

His Cross for Me

His cross for me,
God planned if for His Son.
To set me free,
The work of sin undone.

Oh Christ, your cross with passion we adore,
And for your grace, with faith, we do implore.

His cross for me,
He suffered there alone.
My sin, His grief,
To once for all atone.

Oh Christ, your cross with passion we adore,
And for your grace, with love, we do implore.

His cross for me,
The world is left behind.
Your sure release,
Is all I seek and find.

Oh Christ, your cross, with passion we adore,
And for your grace, with joy, we do implore.

His cross for me,
I daily take it up.
Your strength my plea,
To drink of your sweet cup.

Oh Christ, your cross with passion we adore
And for your grace and mercy we implore.

His cross for me,
Those wounds undid the fall.
The Lamb sets free,
Forever praised by all.

Oh Christ, your cross with passion we adore,
And for your grace, we praise you ever more.

SJH

1

The Cross in History

"Then he released Barabbas for them, but after having Jesus scourged, he handed him over to be crucified."
Matthew 27:26

The "he" in this verse of Scripture is the infamous Pontius Pilate, a brutal and politically powerful man. His true heart is seen clearly through the lens of this greatest event in history—the cross. The response to the cross of Christ is the great revealer of the true heart of every man, not just evil political leaders like Pilate.

Pilate was the fifth in a series of ten Roman prefects or procurators (governors) who ruled Judea in the first century. Judea at that time was a conquered Roman territory. Pilate's was the longest tenure (A.D. 26 to A.D. 36) of all the Roman governors of this unruly province, officially classified as an "Imperial" province because of the frequent occurrences of rebellion there. The ongoing possibility of more rebellion by the Jews loomed large in daily life in Judea.

"Senatorial" provinces, by contrast, were peaceful areas of the Empire. The subjects in those provinces lived in harmony with their Roman masters, dutifully paid their taxes, and obeyed Roman laws. Judea was no such place. If Pilate could have been assigned a position in one of those calmer provinces, how different his life might have been. Instead he was assigned to this backwoods hotbed of rebellion. He was over a thousand miles east across land and sea from Rome, in one of the most distant and difficult corners of the great Empire, probably far from where he wanted to be.

But as the Gospels bear out, Pilate was a hard man and a man of duty. He knew how to deal with rebels. He had already slaughtered some Galileans before Christ's crucifixion because of their rebellion, and even mixed their blood with their sacrifices to terrorize any who might consider a similar path of insurrection. He did not fear confrontation with those under his authority who resisted the control of Rome. In Judea, he *was* Rome. That kind of power is intoxicating to any man, often blurring his moral and ethical judgment.

Perhaps what Pilate most despised in his position as pre-fect were the attempts at manipulating him by the Jewish High Priest and the semi-autonomous ruling body of seventy Jewish elders the High Priest oversaw called the Sanhedrin. He knew they hated Jesus because of His popularity with the people, who viewed Him as a great prophet. Many even viewed him as the Messiah, the future Priest-King prophe-sied about in the Old Testament Scriptures, who would de-liver Israel from all their sin and the oppression of all their enemies. Pilate knew that the Jewish leadership had plotted against Jesus out of pure jealousy and a desire to maintain their own power over their countrymen, with all the trap-pings of wealth and influence their power provided.

As Caiaphas the High Priest had said, it was expedi-ent for one man to die for the entire nation, a prophetic statement, but not as Caiaphas meant it. He meant Jesus was an obstacle to his continued power and it would be good for Jesus to be dead. In contrast, God meant it for the eternal spiritual good of all mankind. As with Pilate, the crucifixion of Jesus brought out the worst in Caiaphas. All he could think about was Jesus as a threat to his current religious power and position. All Pilate could think about was his future in the Roman Empire as a leader. Nothing could stand in the way of that. In this lust for power, he and Caiaphas were alike.

But unlike Caiaphas, Pilate did not want to crucify Je-sus. He found no guilt in Him worthy of death. Then to make matters worse, he was warned by his wife through a dream she had concerning Jesus the night before Christ's trial. She told her husband not to have anything to do with convicting Jesus of any crime. The trial was held the next morning, early on Friday, the day of the Jewish Passover, after the Jews tried and convicted Jesus themselves. They brought Jesus to the Praetorium, part of the palace complex Pilate lived in while in Jerusalem, to seek his official condemnation. The warning from his wife and his own assessment that Christ was innocent prompted Pilate to attempt three times to release Jesus during His trial, which he oversaw. He failed, because he feared losing his position through potential false accusations by the Jewish leaders to the emperor that he was defending someone who claimed to be the king of the Jews.

At one point in the proceedings, he learned that Herod Antipas was in Jerusalem. He was the ruler of Galilee, where Jesus was from, and the son of the late Herod the Great who had attempted to kill Jesus shortly after His birth. Pilate sent Jesus to Herod Antipas, who was staying at his Jerusalem palace, for a ruling on the matter of Christ's guilt or innocence, since Jesus was a Galilean. Herod sent Jesus back, having concluded He was not guilty of death. As with other men of power, this show of confidence by Pilate in Herod that day initiated a friendship between them, resolving a tension between the two rulers that had made them enemies before.

Finally, in frustration and willing to appease the Jewish leaders, Pilate symbolically washed his hands of the matter before the assembled court and gave in to their pleas to crucify Jesus. Nothing but repentance and faith could ever cleanse Pilate from the cowardly miscarriage of justice he committed that day by ordering the crucifixion of Jesus. Secular and church history is relatively silent about Pilate's life after the crucifixion of Jesus, except brief mentions of him of a negative nature by Roman, Jewish, and Christian historians of the time. That relative silence does not bode well for him. Tragically, no repentance and faith by Pilate is reported in any historical source. Any man who rejects Christ and persecutes His followers, like Pilate, will suffer final condemnation in the Court of Heaven, unless he repented of his great sins and trusted Christ as his Savior before his death.

Instead of releasing Jesus, Pilate released a man named Barabbas, a murderer who had participated in an insurrection by the Jews against Rome. That is who the Jews wanted released. There is deep irony in this decision by Pilate since the accusation of the Jews against Jesus was that he was fomenting insurrection as "a new king of Israel." It was Pilate's custom to release one prisoner they requested each year at Passover. He chose a blood-shedding rebel instead of Christ, who he from the evidence believed was innocent of insurrection or any other crime worthy of death. Though Jesus was guilty of no crime, Pilate still had Him scourged, a merciless whipping that left his back and shoulders in ribbons of bloody flesh, and sent Him away to be crucified.

When Jesus reached the hill called Golgotha, meaning the Place of the Skull, the Roman soldiers, led by a centurion, nailed his hands and feet with long, thick iron spikes to a cross in the shape of a lowercase "t." They lifted the cross up, with Christ suspended on it. There he would die slowly, they thought, experiencing the most torturous and humiliating form of capital punishment employed by the Romans in the first century. It was reserved for those in the Empire who were not Roman citizens and had the temerity to violate Roman laws.

Those who died on the cross often succumbed to shock brought on by the scourging prior to it, coupled with the three major puncture wounds caused by the nails, dehydration, lack of food, exposure to the elements, physical exhaustion, and ultimately suffocation caused by the victim's inability to lift himself to breathe while suspended on the cross. Jesus hung on the cross for six hours, from 9:00 am to 3:00 pm, a relatively brief time compared to most. The brevity of the time surprised Pilate when he learned of it. He was of course completely unaware of the crushing burden of the sin of all humankind that Christ was enduring on that simple wooden implement of torture during those six hours. At times in human history, a few hours outweigh a thousand years in significance because of what happens during them. This was certainly true of Christ's six hours on the cross.

During His hours on the cross, Jesus prayed to His Father for the forgiveness of His torturers, spoke to His disciple John and His mother Mary about her care, and told one of the two thieves crucified with him that due to his faith he would be in paradise that day with Him. At one point after hanging for hours on the cross, He cried out in thirst and drank sour wine provided for Him. He then loudly announced He had been forsaken by the Father due to the sin of all men which He was bearing as our substitute.

For half the time Jesus hung on the cross, from 12:00 noon to 3:00 pm, darkness descended on the earth, an act of His Father through His creation symbolic of the spiritual darkness engulfing Christ in His substitutionary death for us. Then suddenly, after hours of agony, Jesus declared triumphantly that He had completed the redemption of all by the shedding of His blood in death, for those who would believe in Him as God and Savior. At the final moment, He cried out, "It is finished. Into Your hands I commend My spirit." Galatians 4:4–5 describes what was achieved on the cross for each of us that day. "But when the fullness of time was come, God sent forth His Son, born of a woman, born under the Law, so that He might redeem those who were under the Law, that we might receive the adoption as sons."

The crucifixion of Christ is the most significant event in human history, the true crossroads for every man, providing the only way of redemption from the slavery of sin and its eternal consequences. It was the greatest crisis, the very central event of the incarnation of Christ. It revealed the depth of the full darkness of men and the full light of God. It was the fullness of time, both in the chronology of events in human history and the significance of what Christ had achieved for all mankind.

Full Historical Record

The full record of Christ's arrest, trials, crucifixion, resurrection, and post-resurrection appearances are found in the New Testament in Matthew 26:36–28:20, Mark 14:32–16:20, Luke 22:29–24:53, John 18:1–21:25, and Acts 1:1–11.

Prayer

"Father, open our eyes to see clearly what happened that day. Bring it all before us as if we were there. May the suffering of our Lord and Savior be vivid to us. Make the envy, cruelty, and injustice of those responsible for this crime leave us aghast at what men will sink to in their evil. Help us recoil at the physical agony Jesus submitted Himself to for us. By the Spirit, fill us with awe and gratitude for the spiritual alienation from you the Lord Jesus was willing to endure for us though He had never sinned Himself. Thank you for sending your Son to achieve redemption for us, the glorious emancipation from sin and its consequences that we can experience as His disciples because of the cross. Thank you for the length and breadth, the height and the depth of the love of Christ shown to us that day, like no other day in human history. Amen."

2

The Cross
in Eternity

*"But with the precious blood of Christ, as of a
lamb without blemish and without spot: who ver-
ily was foreordained before the foundation of the
world, but was manifest in these
last times for you."*
1 Peter 1:19–20

The death and resurrection of Christ to deliver us from our sins was God's plan from the beginning. Christ on the cross was "foreordained before the foundation of the world but was manifest in these last times for you." The cross was never just an alternative plan since God's first plan of continual, uninterrupted fellowship with man had failed through the sinful rebellion of man in the Garden of Eden. God has always known all things, including that the human race would rebel against Him and require a Savior.

But that creates a real logical dilemma whose resolution this side of Heaven seems impossible. If God knew about man's sinful rebellion in advance and the misery and destruction which would result in advance (His omniscience), He could have prevented it by His complete power (His omnipotence). Then why didn't He prevent it? That is a good question to consider because of the humility it requires of us. It is a question that must be left for explanation in eternity by Him. It should simply cause us now to bow in humble recognition that His ways are not our ways and His thoughts are not our thoughts. It is always the unanswered questions about God and His ways that make God a God above us and worthy of worship like no other. That is the ministry of this unanswered question to us.

But what we can fathom now is that God our Father did plan in eternity an actual, physical entrance of His Son into the world to shed His "precious blood." What divine compassion! That blood was infinitely valuable through His perfect sinlessness, "as of a lamb without blemish and without spot," alluding to the requirements of Israel's symbolic worship system. What a final exaltation of His Old Testament revelation is reflected in the words of John the Baptist, who said, "Behold the lamb of God, which taketh away the sins of the world" (John 1:29). God chose precisely the right sacrifice for us, the only one sufficient to redeem us. It was of greater value than all silver or gold. What abundant wisdom, grace, and generosity! He foreordained that Christ would die for us all "before the foundation of the world," before there was a physical world and any men or women in it, showing the priority God placed on the spiritual life and destiny of us all above all else. What foresight! What all-sufficiency! What glory! This we *can* understand, and for this we should offer ceaseless praise.

Prayer

"Keep us, O Lord, from both the temptation and the futile confusion that rise up from our finite thoughts about your ways in salvation. Draw our hearts instead to your greatness, your deep, unfathomable love, your endless compassion and your grace unsurpassed shown us through the cross. Flood our hearts with joy unspeakable and full of glory as we meditate on the Lamb who was slain before the foundation of the world and who now lives forever, interceding for us at your right hand, Father. He alone is worthy of our praise, our time, our riches, and all the days of our lives. Once in eternity with you, when time will be no more, the timing of your conceiving of your plan of redemption through the cross will not concern us, except as a cause for more gratitude and praise. All awareness of and concern for time will be consumed by your presence, your power, and your peace. We will forever be enraptured by undistracted joy in the glorious present with you. Perhaps it will be today. May it be today, Lord, may it be!"

3

The Cross
in Genesis

*"I will put enmity between you and the woman,
and between your seed and her seed; He shall
bruise you on the head, and you
shall bruise him on the heel."*
Genesis 3:15

Genesis 3:15 reports God's words to Satan, embodied as a serpent, after his temptation of Adam and Eve resulting in their fall into sin. This statement is universally recognized by Bible interpreters as the first mention of the cross of Christ in the Bible. At man's first failure through sin, God immediately announces for the first time how this horrendous problem will be resolved.

God starts His explanation of His solution for the curse of sin by saying, "I will put enmity between you and the woman." In this statement, the role of a woman in addressing the problem of sin is presented first. Eve was the first to be tempted and fail through disobedience, but through a woman the great deliverer from sin, Jesus, would come. This is a veiled prophetic allusion to Mary of Nazareth, the mother of Jesus. She was a godly Jewish young woman engaged to marry Joseph, an equally godly young man. The depth of Mary's walk with God is clear from her hymn of praise recorded in Luke 1:46–55 in response to her learning of her role in the entrance of the Christ into the world. Mary was an instrument of God for His glory to bring light into the world in complete contrast to Lucifer, once a cherub whose name meant "Lightbearer." Now he was the epitome of darkness and she the bearer of the Light.

God said that there would be enmity "between your seed and her seed." By this He meant that enmity would exist between Satan's seed and Mary's seed. Satan's seed are the men he would control and by whom he would attempt to kill Jesus. They included Herod the Great, who attempted to kill Jesus at this birth. Later once Christ's ministry began, they included the Pharisees, the Sadducees, and the Herodians. At the end, this group included Annas, the former Jewish High Priest and father-in-law to Caiaphas the Jewish High Priest; the Sanhedrin (the Jewish supreme court made up of 70 Jewish elders); Herod Antipas, the ruler of Galilee and Perea and son of Herod the Great; and finally Pontius Pilate, the Roman governor. Throughout the history of the Church, the enmity between the children of Satan and the children of God has continued because of the opposition of Satan to Christ, His way of salvation, and His rightful kingship over all men and all creation.

Mary's seed was Christ, virgin conceived and virgin born, in fulfillment of Isaiah's prophecy, "'Behold, the virgin shall be with child and bear a son, and she will call His name Immanuel,' which translated means, 'God with us'" (Matthew 1:23, quoting Isaiah 7:14). Because Christ was conceived by the Holy Spirit, the announcing angel Gabriel told Mary, "For that reason the holy Child shall be called the Son of God" (Luke 1:35).

God next said to Eve, "He shall bruise you on the head, and you shall bruise him on the heel." Satan would wound Christ at the cross, part of which was the driving of an iron spike through His heels. The picture here is the only partial effectiveness of these wounds in Satan's attempt to destroy Christ once and for all. Christ would on the other hand bruise Satan on the head, speaking of His complete destruction as the orchestrater of sin and rebellion against God. Satan's meticulous plans against God and His people would ultimately end only in eternal imprisonment in the Lake of Fire. Christ is the triumphant one, the Lamb of God who shed His blood on the cross for our sins and who gives to those who trust Him the gift of eternal life.

Prayer

"Dear Lord, we praise you for your plan of redemption from the beginning. While we grieve over the entrance of sin into the world and its effect in us, we rejoice in your use of a young woman who loved and feared you by whom you entered the world for our salvation. Give us grace to follow her example of submission and obedience to you. Thank you for entering this world to live in perfect obedience and die a perfectly atoning death for us. Help us live today in light of your victory over sin, death, and Satan through the cross and your resurrection. In your almighty and all-knowing name we pray. Amen."

4

The Cross and Providence

"Jesus the Nazarene . . . you nailed to a cross by the hands of godless men and put Him to death. But God raised Him up again."
Acts 2:22–24

The crucifixion of Christ was a human crime, but a divine plan. At Pentecost, Peter preached, "Men of Israel, listen to these words: Jesus the Nazarene, a man attested to you by God with miracles and wonders and signs which God performed through Him in your midst, just as you yourselves know—this Man, delivered over by the predetermined plan and foreknowledge of God, you nailed to a cross by the hands of godless men and put Him to death. But God raised Him up again, putting an end to the agony of death, since it was impossible for Him to be held in its power" (Acts 2:22–24). At the cross, in God's plan, the murderous acts of wicked men became the greatest eternal good for all men.

First, the cross was God's answer for man's greatest problem. While Peter clearly announced at Pentecost the great transgression of the Jewish leaders in plotting the murder of Christ, he added the good news of salvation. He proclaimed, "Repent, and each of you be baptized in the name of Jesus Christ for the forgiveness of your sins and you will receive the Holy Spirit" (Acts 2:38). That day, thousands trusted in the Christ to save them, the very one they before had rejected. What compelled them to faith? The supernatural death of Christ on the cross was compelling. His resurrection from the tomb and His many appearances alive for forty days after the resurrection compelled men to believe. The Spirit-empowered message delivered by Peter and the other disciples about these events for fifty days after the Passover, leading up to Pentecost—and then proclaimed publicly in many languages on that day—pierced the hearts of the multitudes, bringing repentance and faith in Christ.

Second, the cross was caused by the hatred of man but showed God's great power through love. What a demonstration of God's superior wisdom, to show He can turn the greatest tragedy of human iniquity into an unparalleled spiritual triumph for all. What a show of His great power of love that the evil of men inspired by hatred and jealousy may be used by God at Christ's crucifixion and yet He remain holy, untainted by their sin. Our lives in God are made possible through the death of His Son, who bore our sins in His body on the Cross. The Prince of Life tasted death that we may be consumed by His life. The Holy One became sin for us that we may be made the righteousness of God in Him. This was planned in the council of the Trinity as the greatest demonstration of compassionate, selfless sacrifice to be witnessed in all human history. "God is love" (1 John 4:8) and He "demonstrates His own love toward us, in that while we were yet sinners, Christ died for us" (Romans 5:8). "Therefore be imitators of God, as beloved children; and walk in love, just as Christ loved you and gave Himself up for us, an offering and sacrifice to God as a fragrant aroma" (Ephesians 5:1–2).

Prayer

"Dear Father, we praise you for your selfless sacrifice through the Lord Jesus at the cross for us. We thank you Father for your wisdom and your power to use evil to bring the greatest good—our salvation. Our hearts are comforted by this knowledge and made strong in faith, that the evil allowed to touch us each day will bring us only to your goodness in the end. Even the evil intentions of men toward us will transform us and lead us on into the glory of all you are and what we may become for you. In Jesus' name we pray, Amen."

5

Love Displayed through the Cross

"God demonstrates His own love toward us, in that while we were yet sinners, Christ died for us."
Romans 5:8

In what is often called the golden text of the New Testament, learned early by most Christians, the depth of God's love for mankind is summarized. "For God so loved the world that He gave His only begotten Son, that whoever believes in Him shall not perish but have eternal life" (John 3:16). The love of God is by its nature selfless and sacrificial, and the extent of it is astounding. This is the sacrifice of His unique Son, a member of the Trinity with whom He enjoyed fellowship and worship for eternity. To be "only begotten," as Christ is described, does not mean *created* before or above all others; it means *existing* before and above all others, and unlike any other. The loving act of God at the Cross through Jesus, the only begotten Son, will deliver a person from perishing and give that one the gift of eternal life. Instead of torment forever there will be love, joy, hope, and peace forever. What an incomprehensible act of love to provide such a benefit!

Jesus taught in His closing instruction to His disciples before His death that "greater love has no man than this, that one lay down his life for his friends" (John 15:13). The Lord Jesus demonstrated this supreme love. He laid down His life for His friends. He emptied Himself of all His privileges in Heaven from being God, took on human life, and became a servant of mankind (Phil 2:6–7). But He took a step further. The Sovereign of the Universe became obedient to the will of the Father and experienced death, even the death of the cross (Phil 2:8). There was no greater agony, no greater excruciating pain, no more extreme torture, and no more extensive shame than the cross. In summary, it was the worst possible death to die in the first century. Add to this all the sin of every man past, present, and future and the consequent alienation from the Father and He was facing a crushing burden beyond our comprehension. But there is a fact about this that leaves us dumbfounded, utterly stunned. It is found in Romans 5:8.

The remarkable fact is that God did this for us "while we were yet sinners" (Rom 5:8). There was absolutely nothing in any man to commend him to God for such a demonstration of love. In fact, there was the opposite. Parents sacrifice for their children. Employers may sacrifice for good employees, at times. Men may sacrifice for their country to maintain freedom and prosperity. But men do not normally sacrifice for their enemies, those who oppose them, oppose their families, or oppose their own work and prosperity. When the Bible describes men as "sinners," it is describing them as breakers of God's laws, rebels against His rulership, lovers of all kinds of evil, and supremely self-centered, caring only for what is good for them. This is a tragic portrait of mankind as a whole and of every individual man and woman. But God's love prevailed over sin. We deserved death and eternal punishment, but divine love prevailed at the cross.

There is only one right response to this love demonstrated at the cross. "We love, because He first loved us" (1 John 4:19). "By this the love of God was manifested in us, that God sent His only begotten Son into the world so that we might live through Him" (1 John 4:9). Our response to the love shown us on the cross and the great work done there for us is to love God with all our heart, soul, mind, and strength. This is the first and great commandment (Matt 22:36–40; Luke 10:27). And we are to love our "neighbors"; this is the second greatest commandment. This means those we come to know who are in desperate need physically and spiritually, not just family and friends. First among our neighbors, we are to love fellow believers. Jesus said, "This is My commandment, that you love one another, just as I loved you" (John 15:12). "Therefore be imitators of God, as beloved children; and walk in love, just as Christ also loved you and gave Himself up for us, an offering and a sacrifice to God as a fragrant aroma" (Eph 5:1–2).

Prayer

"God of love, open our eyes to see your love fully on the cross through your Son. By your Spirit help us comprehend the length, breadth, height, and depth of it. Work in us what is beyond our desire and our imagination that we may receive it in all fullness. Pour your love into our hearts by your Spirit that we may imitate your love shown through your Son and the death He died for us on Calvary. In the name of Him who is love we pray. Amen."

6

The Lamb of God on the Cross

"Behold the Lamb of God, who takes away
the sin of the world."
John 1:29

While John the Baptist, a cousin of Jesus and six months older than Him, was baptizing in Bethany beyond the Jordan, he described himself to the Jewish leaders as a fulfillment of the prophecy of Isaiah 40:3, "I am a voice of one crying in the wilderness, Make straight the way of the Lord."John said clearly that he was not the Messiah. The very next day he saw Jesus coming to him and said, "Behold the Lamb of God, who takes away the sin of the world "(John 1:29). In this statement he was building on the symbolism of the Old Testament sacrificial worship system, and even before that, the sacrifice of the lamb for the Passover when Israel was delivered from Egypt. Later the same day while standing with two of his disciples, John saw Jesus again and said, "'Behold, the Lamb of God!' The two disciples heard him speak, and they followed Jesus" (John 1:36). From this point forward in the narrative of John's short ministry, he directed attention away from himself to Christ, the Lamb of God. This act is an important example for us in service. Jesus described John as the last in the line of the Old Testament prophets and the greatest of them all, a model for us to follow as servants of the Lamb of God.

John the Baptist was the first in the Gospels to describe Jesus as the Lamb of God. His description of Jesus echoed a major passage in the Old Testament which describes the suffering of our Savior on the cross for our sins—Isaiah 53:1–12. Among the many details of this description, lost men are described as sheep. "All of us like sheep have gone astray; each of us has turned to his own way; but the Lord has caused the iniquity of us all to fall on Him" (Isaiah 53:6). Christ, the Lamb of God, would bear the sins of all the lost sheep of the world, the whole of mankind in their iniquity.

This description of the Lord Jesus also speaks to His

manner, which was characteristic of His life and magnified in His death, a model for us in ministry. Isaiah the prophet wrote, "He was oppressed and He was afflicted, Yet He did not open His mouth; Like a lamb that is led to slaughter, and like a sheep that is silent before its shearers, so He did not open His mouth" (Is 53:7). Christ did not answer the accusations of the Jewish leaders when He was before Pilate, at which Pilate marveled (Mark 15:1–5), nor did He answer the questions of Herod Antipas (Luke 23:9), who subsequently mocked Him and had Him beaten before sending Him back to Pilate. Jesus never reviled or sought revenge against those who opposed Him in His sacrificial ministry. He was meek, gentle, and lowly, as we must be in service (Matt 11:29–30).

John the Apostle wrote the climactic book of the New Testament, the Revelation. In it he describes the end of time as we know it and gives us a glimpse of eternity (Rev 4–22). He had recorded the words of John the Baptist identifying Jesus as the Lamb of God in his gospel, his first great work in the New Testament. In his final great book, the Revelation, he magnifies Christ as the Lamb of God, focusing on His sacrificial death through the shedding of blood. Christ is seen first in the Revelation as our glorified Great High Priest (Rev 1:12–16), but then He appears as the Lamb slain for the sins of men, qualifying Him to take the scroll from the hand of the Father on His throne to begin the just execution of judgment during the Great Tribulation (Rev 5:6–14). We also learn from Revelation 7:9–17 and 14:6–7 that the Tribulation is also a time of great mercy though the time of the just wrath of the Lamb. The whole world hears the gospel during this time and countless multitudes trust Christ as the Lamb that was slain for their sins and their Savior.

What follows is all of Heaven singing praise to Him who was slain and who bought with His blood men for God from every tribe and nation (Rev 5:9–10). To Him they sing, "Worthy is the Lamb that was slain to receive power and riches and wisdom and might and honor and glory and blessing" (Rev 5:12). Similar praise is described as rising from the multitude saved out of the Great Tribulation: "'Salvation to our God who sits on the throne, and to the Lamb.' "These are the ones who come out of the great tribulation, and they have washed their robes and made them white in the blood of the Lamb'" (Rev 7:10, 14).

The New Jerusalem, part of the New Universe in which believers will dwell, is described by John the Apostle: "I saw no temple in it, for the Lord God the Almighty and the Lamb are its temple, and the city has no need of the sun or of the noon to shine on it, for the glory of God has illumined it, and its lamp is the Lamb" (Rev 21:22–23). Only those "written in the Lamb's book of life" (Rev 21:27) will dwell in that light in communion with Him forever. The Lion of the Tribe of Judah, the King of Kings and Lord of Lords, is none other than the Lamb of God "who takes way the sin of the world" (John 1:29). It is His sacrifice as the Lamb that exalts Him as the Lion-King forever.

Prayer

"Lamb of God, we praise you for your meekness in suffering and dying for us. We praise you that you did not call legions of angels to deliver you, but willingly shed your blood. We rejoice in the unity of your truth taught in the Passover deliverance of Israel, the symbolic and prophetic worship taught in the law of Moses, and in your sacrificial death on the cross through the shedding of your blood. We bow before you in adoration for purchasing us with your precious blood. Give us grace to silently bear wrong, as you did during your trials before both religious and political officials for our good. We thank you that our names are written in the Lamb's book of life so we may know you as our Lamb-Shepherd forever. Amen."

7

Our Priest-Sacrifice Forever through the Cross

"For it was fitting for us to have such a high priest, holy, innocent, undefiled, separated from sinners and exalted above the heavens; who does not need daily, like those high priests, to offer up sacrifices, for His own sins and then for the sins of the people, because this He did once for all when He offered up Himself."
Hebrews 7:26, 27

The Book of Hebrews develops in detail the unique role of the Lord Jesus Christ as our High Priest. His high priesthood for us was prophesied in Psalm 11:4 where the Psalmist wrote, "You are a priest forever according to the order of Melchizedek," (quoted about Christ in Hebrews 7:17). This description of Christ was an allusion to the historical figure Melchizedek, a priest of the Most High God who welcomed Abram back with a special blessing after a great military victory (Genesis 14:17-20). Abram acknowledged this priest's greatness before God by giving him a tenth of the spoils taken in this just war to free his nephew Lot and the people of Sodom, who had been kidnapped by the armies of a confederation of five pagan kings.

Melchizedek was not of the Aaronic priesthood spoken of in the Law of Moses since he lived before God gave Moses the Law for the children of Israel. Christ, like Melchizedek, was unique as a priest in that He was of the tribe of Judah, not of the tribe of Levi and a descendant of Aaron, the brother of Moses and first high priest of Israel. But His uniqueness extends far beyond His physical heritage.

Christ, unlike all other high priests before Him, was without sin. The author of Hebrews piles up terms, one upon the other, to emphasize this truth. He describes Christ as "innocent, undefiled, separated from sinners, and exalted above the heavens" (Hebrews 7:26). There was no guilt in Jesus ("innocent"), no moral pollution in Him ("undefiled"), no impurity by conforming to the way of sinners ("separated from sinners") and completely apart from all that is mundane and profane ("exalted above the heavens). The Lord Jesus didn't need to offer up sacrifices "for His own sins." He had none.

Christ's high priesthood for us is also unique in that He offered Himself as the sacrifice for our sins, not the sacrificial death and blood of animals as described in the Law of Moses. These were all only symbolic sacrifices, figuratively representative of what Christ would do one day on the cross for us (Hebrews 9:6-10). Another element of the uniqueness of Christ's sacrifice on the cross was that it was once for all for all men. The sacrifice didn't need to be repeated daily for the sins of men. "Otherwise, He would have needed to suffer often since the foundation of the world; but now once at the consummation of the ages He has been manifested to put away sin by the sacrifice of Himself" (Hebrews 9:26). Christ in His all-sufficiency accomplished our salvation, "once for all, having obtained redemption" for us (Hebrews 9:12).

Once Christ died on the Cross, he then arose again and ascended back to Heaven after 40 days of ministry among His disciples. Seated at the right hand of God in Heaven, our Great High Priest-Sacrifice makes intercession for us as our compassionate, sympathizing High Priest who was tempted in all the ways we have been tempted, but without sinning (Hebrews 4:15). He advocates with the Father on our behalf when we fail through sin (1 John 2:1-2). His presence with God as our High Priest motivates us to fellowship with God through prayer daily for fresh help and renewed hope. "Therefore let us draw near with confidence to the throne of grace, so that we may receive mercy and find grace to help in time of need (Hebrews 4:16). He hears our cries for cleansing and for strength to live to honor Him and will grant us what we need for both —His mercy and His grace.

Prayer

"Lord Jesus, we praise you for your uniqueness as our High Priest at the right hand of the Father. You are like none other, before you or since. We thank you for your all-sufficient sacrifice for us on the cross and your presentation of yourself to the Father on our behalf. We confess that our change-ableness leaves us in awe over the single, unchanging power of your sacrifice on the cross, once for all. We rejoice in your present ministry of intercession for us at the right hand of the Father based on the sacrifice of yourself. We plead for your mercy for our sins and for your grace we need to serve today, merited by you through your sacrificial death for us. In your name as our High Priest we pray. Amen.

8

Christ's Example of Suffering on the Cross

"For you have been called for this purpose, since Christ also suffered for you, leaving you an example for you to follow His steps."
1 Peter 2:21

In the verse immediately preceding 1 Peter 2:21, Peter wrote, "For what credit is there if, when you sin and are harshly treated, you endure it with patience? But if when you do what is right and suffer for it, you patiently endure it, this finds favor with God" (1 Pet 2:20). Then Peter unfolds the suffering Christ endured on the cross as our example for how to suffer when we are mistreated for doing what is right according to the Scriptures. This may be living a godly lifestyle before others, testifying to others of our faith in Christ, or openly standing against some prevalent sin of the culture in which we live. We may experience verbal abuse, physical abuse, being ostracized because we are Christians, being left out of social events in our community, or missing opportunities for advancement at our job.

Christ was the perfect example of how to suffer for doing what is right. Nothing was more right than His death on the cross for the sins of the world. This benevolent, completely self-sacrificial act by Christ was totally undeserved by the world of lost men. It was misunderstood by many at the time and resulted in their abuse of Him. How did He respond to this, providing a pattern for us to follow when we suffer for Him?

First, the Scriptures describe Him in these circumstances as One "who committed no sin" (1 Pet 2:22). This sweeping comment makes it clear that not in the smallest way, internally or externally, did Christ's suffering provoke Him to violate God's law. He remained completely holy in attitudes, words, and actions. Others may find an excuse in the abuse they receive from others for an equally abusive response, but not Christ.

Second, Peter wrote of Jesus, "Nor was any deceit found in His mouth" (1 Pet 2:22). Jesus did not utter a single syllable that would mislead those persecuting Him, causing them to abuse Him less, even though He did not deserve their vicious words and actions. He fully owned who He was and what He was doing while He was suffering before and during His crucifixion.

Third, Peter said that "while being reviled, He did not revile in return" (1 Pet 2:23). The High Priest spoke disparagingly of Christ, calling Him a blasphemer for claiming He was the Son of God. The Sanhedrin joined their leader, the High Priest, by mocking Christ. Pilate's soldiers mocked Him because He claimed to be the King of the Jews, as did the soldiers of Herod. The crowds observing the crucifixion mocked Him, as did both of the criminals from their crosses on either side of Christ, until one of them later trusted Christ to save him before he died. In response to all this verbal abuse, Jesus uttered not a single word of condemnation against them. He said nothing negative to them at all.

Fourth, "while suffering, He uttered no threats, but kept entrusting Himself to Him who judges righteously" (1 Pet 2:23). Jesus remained steadfast in His trust of the Father while completing His will to die for the sins of the world. In truth, He could have immediately called for the aid of thousands of angels to destroy all those who were physically and verbally abusing Him. He not only didn't call for such help, He didn't even threaten those who were sinning against Him. There was no revenge planned against those who were against Him, only mercy, grace, compassion, and love. This was the example of Christ for us in how to live when suffering for righteousness.

Prayer

"Father, thank you for giving us your Spirit to strengthen us in our weakness when suffering for righteousness. We exult in you for your abundant grace to exercise self-control when our flesh cries out for revenge, retaliation. Lord Jesus, how we praise you for your masterful modeling, your perfect example of righteous suffering. In you we find both the pattern and power to rejoice in our suffering for your name's sake. As we abide in you, help us abound much in the fruit of longsuffering when we are provoked mercilessly by others. Pour out upon us your meekness when we are abused by those over us in authority. Grant to us the peace that passes all understanding rather than a heart of war toward those who misuse and abuse us. May we suffer like you, always for your glory. We pray, relying on your strength alone, not our own. Amen."

9

The Christian's Suffering Like His at the Cross

"that I may know Him and the power of His resurrection and the fellowship of His sufferings, being conformed to His death"
Philippians 3:10

The purpose of Christ's suffering on the cross was to save all men from sin. "For Christ died for sins once for all, the just for the unjust, so that He might bring us to God, having been put to death in the flesh, but made alive in the spirit" (1 Pet 3:18). Like Jesus, our purpose should be to see men come to Christ in repentance and faith as their Savior from sin and the Lord of their lives daily. Whatever sacrifices we are called upon to make, like Christ, are for that purpose. We are to desire to know by experience those sacrifices: "that I may know Him . . . and the fellowship of His sufferings, being conformed to His death" (Phil 3:10). This will lead to the full experience of resurrection power spiritually in this life. In the end, we will experience our physical resurrection in new bodies. We must arm ourselves with a clear view of what the sufferings of Christ entailed, which culminated in His death. We should not avoid those sufferings but rather embrace them. What were the sufferings of Christ, climaxing in the cross?

First, like Christ, we must expect rejection by our own people. Christ experienced the rejection of His own nation, who were looking for the Messiah. The Messiah was the future anointed prophet-priest-king foretold in the Old Testament. He would deliver Israel from all political and spiritual oppression. Christ experienced some rejection from His own family during His public ministry, particularly from His own brothers, "For not even His brothers were believing in Him" (John 7:5).

Next, those in His hometown of Nazareth rejected Him not only as the Messiah but even as a prophet. They attempted to kill Him after He preached in their synagogue the first time because of His honest description of their wrong attitude (Luke 4:16–30).

Then, while Christ enjoyed massive responsiveness from the common people in Palestine during His ministry because of His teaching and healing, those in official leadership in the nation rejected Him. Near the end of His public ministry after describing the rejection of the religious leaders of the nation, He said, "Jerusalem, Jerusalem, who kills the prophets and stones those who are sent to her! How often I wanted to gather your children together the way a hen gathers her chicks under her wings and you were unwilling. Behold, your house is being left to you desolate" (Matt 24:37–38).

Second, like Christ, we must expect opposition from governmental authorities to Christ and the message of the cross. Both Herod Antipas and Pontius Pilate, Roman-appointed governors in Palestine, came into league with the religious leaders to both try Him legally and put Him to death. Luke wrote, "And Herod with his soldiers, after treating Him with contempt and mocking Him, dressed Him in a gorgeous robe and sent Him back to Pilate" (Luke 23:11). John records the final outcome of Pilate's deliberations over Jesus. Pilate, after having Jesus scourged (Matt 27:26), said, "Behold, your King! . . . . So he then handed Him over to them to be crucified" (John 19:14, 16).

Third, like Christ, we must expect the worst physical suffering. This is what the cross and crucifixion represented in the first century Roman Empire. It was the culmination of the physical suffering that Jesus was subjected to throughout His ministry. Christ knew all the deprivations of a constantly itinerant ministry, traveling away from His home base in Capernaum. He knew the discomfort of unfamiliar surroundings, hunger, thirst, and fatigue from extreme work. But when His trials began, the physical suffering became more and more intense. The Sanhedrin and their servants holding him in custody mocked and beat Him (Luke 22:63–65). Both Herod's and Pilate's soldiers beat Him, mocked Him, kept striking Him on the head with a reed, and wove a crown of large thorns which they crushed down on His head (Luke 23:11; John 19:1–2). After Pilate had Jesus scourged, the soldiers took Him to Golgotha and crucified Him, nailing Him to the cross with long iron spikes through his hands and feet. Finally, one soldier even pierced Jesus through the side with a spear to insure He was dead (John 19:34).

As servants of Christ, we are not greater than our Master. To spread the gospel and build the Church requires sacrifice, real suffering, in time, energy, material possessions, peace, and safety. Being a true follower of Jesus is not meant to be a life of comfort, light work, and ease. In Christian life and experience, resurrection to newness of life always comes after the death of the cross. We must take up our cross daily and follow Him.

Prayer

"Oh God, by your Spirit give us wisdom to know and walk the true path of discipleship. Help us understand that life always comes after death. Give us eyes to see that the path is narrow, upward, and hard. Guard us, Lord, from craving comfort and ease. Deliver us from shunning the cross-life of suffering and death for the good of others and your glory. Cause our hearts to burn with joy as you open our minds to the Word to understand the path of suffering required for your truth and your name's sake. You are our full joy. Give us rejoicing in trials and in the suffering of the cross as you perfect us through endurance. Amen."

10

The Christian Crucified with Christ

"I have been crucified with Christ; and it is no longer I who live, but Christ lives in me; and the life which I now live in the flesh I live by faith in the Son of God, who loved me and gave Himself up for me"
Galatians 2:20

Christ died at a specific time and place in history on a hill called Golgotha, in Jerusalem, in the first century A.D. It was a real, one-time, historical event. But there comes another moment when that event in history may become the most powerful event in the present for any man, woman, boy, or girl. Irrespective of the century, year, day, or hour, the full impact of the cross in a life-changing way is experienced by the one exercising faith personally in Christ for salvation. On the other hand, those who do not exercise saving faith receive no eternal benefit from the death of Christ for all. None.

Describing his own experience in Galatians 2:20, Paul states, "I have been crucified with Christ." This means that at that moment of saving faith in the death and resurrection of Christ for his sins, the significance of Christ's death in history rushed forward to the present for him. That happened on the Damascus Road for Paul. This is true for all who exercise saving faith, no matter where they are and when they live. The guilt for our sins is removed forever at that moment. The power of our sin nature to control us is crushed permanently at that moment. The gift of eternal life is imparted.

Through His death, we are no longer bound to live for our own sinful desires, ambitions and inclinations because "it is no longer I who live," as Paul said, describing himself as an example of all who believe. We have great hope because "Now if we have died with Christ, we believe that we shall also live with Him" (Rom 6:8).

Galatians 2:20 says that He is in us to help us. As Paul put it, "Christ lives in me." This is accomplished by the Lord Jesus through the Holy Spirit, sent by the Father and Son, who dwells in the heart and body of every believer from the moment of their salvation (Rom 8:9; 1 Cor 12:13). The Spirit represents Christ in us perfectly as God. He is even called the "Spirit of Christ" in Romans 8:9 and the "Spirit of the Son" in Galatians 4:6.

In the words of the text, "The life which I now live in the flesh, I live by faith in the Son of God." This means a constant, abiding trust in Christ every day we are alive as Christians, about all the great and small details and decisions of life.

Christ demonstrated His great heart of complete self-sacrifice for us, which is His love, by offering Himself as our sacrifice for sin on the cross. Paul described Christ as the one "who loved me and gave himself up for me." There is no greater love than this (John 15:13).

Prayer

"Oh Lord, we praise you that in your perfect plan to save us you caused your death on the cross that day to transform all who have saving faith. Your death was the death of sin in us, giving us the power to resist it and follow you. Thank you for interceding for us every moment, every day at the right hand of the Father so we can have victory over sin. We rejoice in your presence with us by faith through your Spirit today. Amen."

11

The Christian Bearing His Own Cross

"If anyone wishes to come after Me, he must deny himself, and take up his cross daily and follow Me."
Luke 9:23

Since the work of Christ on the cross is central to our faith as disciples, it is not surprising that Christ would use the same instrument to describe what living the life of a true disciple must be like. In Luke 9:23, the three descriptions of that life are interdependent and inseparable, with cross bearing at the heart of the statement by Jesus.

The Lord Jesus presents this statement as a condition by beginning with the clause, "If anyone wishes to come after me." The invitation is to be a disciple, which means to become a follower-learner of Christ. This should begin at the moment of saving faith, and it is to continue throughout the believer's life. Christians fail or succeed to varying degrees in their discipleship, depending on the extent to which they meet this three-fold condition.

First, the disciple must "deny himself." His own desires, plans, ambitions, and aspirations must be set aside, freeing his life for following the Master. A personal agenda that includes preoccupation with self-advancement, accumulating material wealth and possessions, constant ease, and personal pleasure disqualify a believer from serious discipleship. But if he resolves daily to put these aside, he has the prospect of a fruitful spiritual experience as a follower of Jesus.

Second, and at the heart of this three-fold condition, is for the disciple to "take up his cross daily." On the cross, Christ bore the sins of men. The disciple must be willing to bear the burden of reaching the lost for whom Christ died on the cross. His life's message must be that of redemption from sin through the work of Christ on the cross. As Paul said it, "For I determined to know nothing among you except Jesus Christ and Him crucified" (1 Cor 2:2). He later reiterated this idea saying, "For we do not preach ourselves but Christ Jesus as Lord, and ourselves your bond-servants for Jesus sake" (1 Cor 4:5). He knew that "the word of the cross is foolishness to those who are perishing, but to us who are being saved it is the power of God" (1 Cor 1:18). This bearing of the message of the cross may mean real suffering brought on by persecution. The cross was the place of Christ's suffering as our Savior. We should respond in kind by bearing our cross for Him.

The disciple must also bear the burden of his cross in another way. He must be ready always to bear the burden of the sins of fellow believers when they fail. Jesus taught this through his illustration of washing the disciples' feet at the last Passover meal. Later, Paul further explained this in Galatians 6:1–2 when he said, "Brethren, even if anyone is caught in any trespass, you who are spiritual, restore such a one in a spirit of gentleness; each one looking to yourself, so that you too will not be tempted. Bear one another's burdens, and thereby fulfill the law of Christ." Delivering fellow believers from the enslavement of sin is part of what Christians do in response to the freedom from sin Christ purchased for believers on the cross. The fact that we are to take up our cross "daily" reminds us that we will have to renew this resolve every day.

The third element of the three-fold condition of discipleship Christ said is "to follow me." The pattern of life of the true disciple of Jesus is obedience. What He says we do. The disciple knows and loves the commands of God written in the Word. They are not a burden to him but the way of joy. They are his chief means of showing his love for God. Through them he shows God his full submission to His will, just as Jesus showed His full submission to the will of the Father all the way to the cross. Beyond obeying the explicit commands of the Word are the challenges of applying the Word to life. This may mean following Him away from family, into the ministry, away from his own culture, and even to a different nation who needs the truth of the gospel.

Prayer

"Lord, as we bow before you, we ask for the grace to meet this three-fold condition to be your faithful disciples. Free us from our selfishness for a life of self-denial. Give us strength to take up our cross, following your example of selfless sacrifice to deliver men from sin. Fill us with love for your Word and determination to obey you as we follow you. Open the way for us to go wherever you would have us go, to do whatever you would have us do for your glory. Amen."

12

The Death of Sinful Desire through the Cross

"Now those who belong to Christ have crucified the flesh with its passions and desires."
Galatians 5:24

This statement in Galatians 5:24 follows the listing of the works of the flesh and the fruit of the Spirit presented by Paul in Galatians 5:16–23. In it, he gives a conclusive reason why it is possible for the believer not to be dominated by the works of the flesh but to live life directed by the Spirit day by day, obeying the commands of Christ and being conformed to His image. When we trusted Christ's work on the cross, our "flesh" was crucified. Since we know that our physical bodies did not die when we trusted Christ as Savior and our inclination to sin did not stop, what does this mean?

The word "flesh" in the New Testament can mean our physical bodies. It also may mean our sinful human nature, which remains with us even after we are born again and indwelled by the Holy Spirit. The contexts in which the term is used help us understand which meaning is intended by the authors of Scripture. Sometimes a passage seems to combine the two meanings, since our sinful desires often find expression through our physical bodies. Romans 6:12 is an example of this where Paul writes, "Therefore do not let sin reign in your mortal body so that you obey its lusts." In Galatians 5:24, however, the "flesh" means our ongoing inclination to sin, not our physical body.

Our sinful nature shows itself in us through our "passions and desires" (Gal 5:24). In this verse, the word "passions" refers to our spiritually diseased condition. We all have what could be called a sort of spiritual cancer of the heart, which will not be fully eradicated until we are glorified in Christ's presence because of His work on the cross. Every day as we struggle with sin, we are reminded of the importance of the work He did there for us. Out of our diseased condition rise all kinds of sinful "desires." We want what we should not want, even as believers in Christ, and consequently do what we should not do. James warns, "But each one is tempted when he is carried away and enticed by his own lust. Then when lust has conceived, it gives birth to sin; and when sin is accomplished, it brings forth death. Do not be deceived, my beloved brethren" (James 1:14–16). The word "lust" in these verses is the same word translated "desires" in Galatians 5:24.

So, if our spiritual cancer of the heart, our sin nature, remains and we still have all kinds of sinful desires as a result, in what sense have our "passions and desires" been crucified? Paul answered this question when he wrote Romans 6:6: "Knowing this, that our old self was crucified with Him, in order that our body of sin might be done away with, so that we would no longer be slaves to sin." The power of our "passions and desires" to control us was put to death. We no longer must give in to our sin nature and the desires that rise out of it. "For he who has died is freed from sin" (Rom 6:7). "And having been freed from sin, you became slaves of righteousness" (Rom 6:18). Through Christ, we now can reject every desire to sin and gladly obey every command of God. "But now having been freed from sin and enslaved to God, you derive your benefit, resulting in sanctification [being made holy], and the outcome, eternal life" (Rom 6:22).

Prayer

"Lord Jesus, what a glorious reality that sin in us has been defeated. It is crucified never to rise to destroy us and condemn us eternally. It no longer reigns supreme over us, causing us to rebel and sin each day. Bring this reality to the forefront of our thinking hour by hour, especially in the hour of temptation. Remind us that going the way of sin is like wrapping our arms around a dead and decaying body, making us filthy and full of corruption. We praise you that when you died for our sins, you put our sinful passions and desires to death for today, every day, and forever, through our faith in you. Amen."

13

The Death of the World through the Cross

*"But may it never be that I would boast except in
the cross of our Lord Jesus Christ, through which
the world has been crucified to me,
and I to the world."*
Galatians 6:14

The centerpiece of Paul's confidence as a believer was the work of the Lord Jesus Christ on the Cross. Among the many remarkable things accomplished for us there was the crucifixion of the world to us and us to the world. This means that Christ's power at the Cross crushed the invincibility of the world's hold on us as an external influence and crushed our desire for it which rises in our hearts as we are influenced by the law of sin resident in us.

But what is "the world" referring to in this passage? What is it *exactly*? In the opening chapter of Galatians Paul spoke of Christ, "who gave Himself for our sins so that He might rescue us from this *present evil age*, according to the will of our God and Father" (Gal 1:4, italics added). The world is this present evil age. It is the antithesis of the Kingdom of God to which the Christian belongs, serving the King, Christ. It is the Enemy's territory in which we are called to serve until Christ returns for us. The "world" is Satan's kingdom, manifested in human culture by political, philosophical, and religious views and behavior that deny and seek to undermine the authority of the true God and His Word. It offers satisfaction to all men, including believers, through physical appetites and comforts ("the lusts of the flesh"), through the mind by what can be seen and learned ("the lust of the eyes"), and through the satisfaction that comes from achievements leading to self-elevation compared to others ("the pride of life") (1 John 2:15-17). In Romans, Paul urges that believers "not be conformed to this world, but be transformed by the renewing of your mind, so that you may prove what the will of God is, that which is good and acceptable and perfect" (Rom 12:2). He is warning that the present age can be like a mold surrounding you and attempting to crush you into its form. The only way to avoid that is to have your thinking and desires transformed by the revelation of God, His Word.

The reality is that at the cross the world's power to shape us was undone. Now we may and must live in that reality by refusing its power and submitting to the teaching of Scripture. We can refuse the world's power because at the cross our desires for the world were crushed in their controlling power. We, like Paul, were "crucified to the world." We must not allow our sin nature, which lives on in us until we see Christ, to breathe life into the dead corpse of worldly desires resident in our hearts. They must remain dead and buried as we believe in what was accomplished for us at the cross by Christ.

Prayer

"Our God and Heavenly Father, as Jesus prayed, 'I do not ask you to take them out of the world, but to keep them from the evil one. They are not of the world, even as I am not of the world' (John 17:18). So please, we beg you Father, keep us from the Evil One and his sinister temptations in this present evil age. Open our hearts to your truth that will transform us and keep us from conforming to the desires of the world. Sanctify us by your truth, which is your Word. Empower us to go into the world to deliver those imprisoned by it that they may know the truth. It is only the truth that will make them free. We ask this in the name of Jesus. Amen."

14

Strange Opposition to the Cross

"And he was stating the matter plainly. And Peter took Him aside and began to rebuke Him."
Mark 8:32

This verse of Scripture raises a question. What matter had Jesus just been speaking plainly to the disciples about? The answer is in the preceding verse: "And He began to teach them that the Son of Man must suffer many things and be rejected by the elders and the chief priests and the scribes and be killed, and after three days rise again" (Mark 8:31).

This instruction occurred immediately after Jesus asked the disciples who men said He was. To this Peter responded, "You are the Christ" (Mark 8:29). Matthew's fuller account says that Peter said, "You are the Christ, the Son of the living God" (Matt 16:16). Peter understood that Jesus was the promised Messiah and the divine Son of God, God incarnate. Jesus then explained, "Blessed are you, Simon Barjona, because flesh and blood did not reveal this to you, but My Father who is in heaven" (Matt 16:17). Peter had received his understanding of Jesus' true nature directly from God. This makes Peter's objection to Christ's explanation of His coming death even more strange.

Matthew records Peter's complete statement to Jesus after Christ revealed His coming death at the hands of the Jewish leaders: "Peter took Him aside and began to rebuke Him, saying, 'God forbid it. Lord! This shall never happen to You'" (Matt 16:22). At this point, the leader of the twelve disciples did not have a clear understanding about how Christ would achieve redemption for man, even though he clearly knew who He was. This is only one of the times in the Gospels, and there are several, when Jesus explained His coming death to His disciples and they did not understand it at all. This failure reveals to us that even the most dedicated followers of Christ may lack knowledge they should have and behave very badly as a result. This is a strong motivation to watch and pray for illumination of the truth so that we do not fall into the temptation of wrong thinking, sinful words, and evil actions because we did not know what we should have known.

Jesus' reaction to Peter offers a sober warning to all of us. "But he turned and said to Peter, 'Get behind Me, Satan! You are a stumbling block to Me; for you are not setting your mind on God's interests, but man's.'" Here is a faithful disciple, truly a follower of Jesus, objecting to his Master's plan concerning the cross. What is worse, Peter had come under the influence of Satan in his statement and was opposing Christ's purposes and God's interests in rescuing mankind from sin. Why? What caused this egregious misjudgment and statement by Peter? He had become concerned about "man's interests."

The temptation to become concerned about "man's interests" in the outworking of our walk with Christ as a disciple always waits to devour us like a lion waiting to pounce and consume. That the way of redemption should involve betrayal, arrest, abuse, and complete self-sacrifice through brutal murder is just unthinkable when you become concerned about "man's interests." Our interests are often sadly in happiness, material comfort, ease, and outward success in ministry, evidenced by the drawing of vast crowds of people. The development of complex, extensive ministries with magnificent facilities viewed as excellent by the world's standards can strangely become our aim. Demonstrating great power and influence over men appeals to our sinful nature. It is a lust of the world, which is called "the pride of life." We know from the conversations the twelve had shortly before Jesus's death that they were confused about their future. They wanted the greatness of authority over others in Christ's future kingdom. Christ taught them this was not His way, but rather the path of lowly, spiritual service to all. Jesus said that the last shall be first and the first shall be last. A humble, self-effacing life of ministry to others is the Christ life.

The path of selfless service begins with embracing the sacrifice of the cross. It continues by taking up your cross daily in sacrificial service. It culminates in losing your life for Him that you may gain it in its true value, which is spiritual and eternal, not material and temporal.

Prayer

"Lord Jesus, we magnify you for your selfless, sacrificial work through the cross. Forgive us for failing to comprehend the true way of discipleship, that it is the way of cross bearing. Open our hearts to a full understanding of the selfless sacrifice required of us. Fill us with desire for what is spiritual not physical, what is eternal not temporal, what is giving not receiving. Give us a thirst for humble service. Remove from us all desire for exaltation among men. May we crave only the last place, the lowest place, the small place, the obscure place, the place of greatest ministry to all that you bring to us. In this we will find greatest blessing. This we ask through your mercy. Amen."

15

Redemption through the Cross

*"In Him we have redemption through His blood,
the forgiveness of our trespasses, according to the
riches of His grace which He lavished on us."*
Ephesians 1:7–8a

Human slavery was common in the Roman Empire in the first century, so the idea of redemption was well known. In the language of the New Testament, to redeem someone was a commercial transaction, buying them out of slavery into freedom. As believers, we are redeemed from spiritual slavery by Christ through faith in His death as our Savior.

Before placing saving faith in Christ, you were enslaved to a position of condemnation by the law of God. You were a guilty lawbreaker without hope of freedom until Christ came in the fullness of time "that He might redeem those who were under the Law" (Gal 4:5). You were also a slave to sin itself, unable to live a life free of it. This does not mean that you committed every kind of sin to the worst possible degree before your salvation. But it does mean that you had no power to keep from sinning. Christ "gave Himself for us to redeem us from every lawless deed, and to purify for Himself a people for His own possession, zealous for good deeds" (Titus 2:14). Further, you were also enslaved by Satan until Christ through His death "might render powerless him who had the power of death, that is, the devil, and might free those who through fear of death were subject to slavery all their lives" (Heb 2:14–15).

As the one mediator between God and men, Christ "gave Himself as a ransom for all" (1 Tim 2:6). He paid the ultimate price to free us from spiritual slavery. "In Him we have redemption through His blood" shed during His death on the cross (Eph 1:7). You were not "redeemed with perishable things like silver and gold from your futile way of life," from the sinful lifestyle learned from your unsaved families and the culture around you (1 Pet 1:18). It was the "precious blood, as of a lamb unblemished and spotless, the blood of Christ" that redeemed us (1 Pet 1:19). Through His blood we have forgiveness for our sins by His "grace which he

lavished on us" (Eph 1:8a). There is now no eternal condemnation for our sins, and we may receive daily spiritual
cleansing through His blood by the confession of our sins.
"But if we walk in the Light, as He Himself is in the Light,
we have fellowship with one another, and the blood of Jesus His son cleanses us from all sin . . . . If we confess our
sins, He is faithful and just to forgive us our sins and to
cleanse us from all unrighteousness" (1 John 1:7–9).

Our purchase out of spiritual slavery does not result in
independence. We are now owned by God as His servants
and treated as sons in His family. Since "you have been
bought with a price, therefore glorify God in your body"
through a life of moral purity (1 Cor 6:19). This purchase
price and our new position in God's household should
motivate us not only to purity but to be "zealous of good
deeds" (Titus 2:14). "For we are His workmanship, created
in Christ Jesus for good works, which God prepared beforehand so that we would walk in them" (Eph 2:10). As
the twenty-four elders before the throne of God in Heaven
sang to Christ before His work in Revelation as the Great
Judge, our hearts should be lifted up daily in praise to
Christ: "Worthy are You to take the book and to break its
seals; for You were slain, and purchased for God with Your
blood men from every tribe and tongue and people and nation. You have made them to be a kingdom and priests to
our God; and they will reign upon the earth" (Rev 5:9–10).

Prayer

"Lord Jesus, we lift our hearts in adoration to you for your great work on the cross as the Lamb of God, shedding your blood for our redemption. We praise you that through your blood we can know cleansing from sin every day. Give us eyes to see and ears to hear your commands to live a life of physical and spiritual purity in daily response to the great price you paid for our spiritual freedom. Our hearts overflow with joy over the reality of our freedom from the condemnation of the Law, the power of sin, and the Devil's enslavemment of us through the fear of death. Thank you for buying us out of slavery to the glorious spiritual liberty we enjoy as your servant-sons forever. Amen."

16

Propitiation through the Cross

"In this is love, not that we loved God, but that He loved us and sent His Son to be the propitiation for our sins."
1 John 4:10

Propitiation is not a frequently used word in the New Testament about Christ's work on the cross, appearing in only three verses, but is an important *concept* that appears often in its pages. It is one of the great works of Christ for us that insures we are the objects of God's constant love and care. We are not the objects of His wrath.

Propitiation is different from the other eternal spiritual transactions that occurred at the cross. In it, God is both the One that is propitiated and the One who propitiates, not man. Propitiation describes what God did for Himself and within the Trinity for the salvation of mankind. The result is a magnificent demonstration of the character of our God and how the extremes of His character come into perfect balance for our good in our salvation.

Propitiation is an idea that finds its roots in the sacrificial worship system of the Old Testament, but in this case God's just wrath against sin is satisfied by the payment of Christ's blood, not the blood of lambs, goats, or bulls. The Lord Jesus was "displayed publicly as a propitiation by His blood through faith" (Rom 3:25). To follow the analogy of the Old Testament sacrificial system, the cross was the altar on which the Lamb of God shed His blood for us.

Jesus anticipated with agony the prospect of bearing the wrath of God for sin as our sacrifice. Three times while He prayed in the Garden of Gethsemane before His arrest He said, "My Father, if it is possible, let this cup pass from Me; yet not as I will, but as You will" (Matt 26:39, 42, 44). At perhaps the darkest moment while suffering as the object of the just wrath of God on the cross for sin, Jesus cried out, "My God, My God, why have You forsaken me?" (Matt 27:46). He, God the Son, knew complete alienation from God the Father as He bore our sins. The Father was fully satisfied with this sacrifice. He was propitiated by the propitiation He Himself provided through Christ.

In this indescribable, incomprehensible act of self-sacrifice, "He loved us and sent His Son to be the propitiation for our sins" (1 John 4:10). Only the great depths of the mercy of God could find the way to satisfy His own just wrath for sin. His own selfless, endless mercy demonstrated by the offering up of Himself as the eternal sacrifice for us was the way.

We rest forever in this truth—His propitiating love guarantees His unchanging kindness toward us as our Father. We bow in respectful awe of Him. We fear His correction as our Father, but know it is never meant to bring our destruction through wrath. It is only meant to increase our holiness (Heb 12:10). Whenever He frowns on us, we know that it is only from a divine heart stricken with deep sadness over our failure through sin. He will never leave us or forsake us. Nothing can separate us from His love in Christ Jesus, who is our propitiation, once for all, forever.

Prayer

"Oh Father, thank you that you are slow to anger, full of abundant lovingkindness, endless in compassion, and gracious toward us. You found a way in mercy to turn your wrath away from us but to be true to your justice. By this, you saved us. Lord Jesus, thank you for your perfect obedience in submitting to the will of the Father for us on the cross, serving as the "propitiation for our sins, and not ours only but the sins of the whole world" (1 John 2:2). Our hearts overflow in grateful praise for the unimaginable pain you suffered, the worst alienation from the Father ever known as the object of His wrath, that we might live every day in the presence and favor of God. This is joy unspeakable, fullness of glory! This is a message worth bearing to all, that you are the propitiation for the sins of the whole world. Help us boldly bear that message for your glory, we pray. Amen."

17

Imputation through the Cross

"He made Him who knew no sin to be sin on our behalf, so that we might become the righteousness of God in Him."
2 Corinthians 5:21

The New Testament idea of imputation is one drawn from the first century world of business, and more specifically, accounting. Like today, if money was paid for a service or a product, that money was credited to the person's account as paid toward the amount due. It was recorded and that record represented what had been paid as certainly as the physical money itself that had been given. If the money paid was for a debt, the record showed the amount paid, in writing. The payment of the debt was "imputed" to the debtor's account.

Like the other eternal transactions performed by Christ at the cross for us, imputation adds yet another layer of depth to the truth about our salvation. It becomes yet another cause of daily joy for the believer. At the cross, imputation occurred for us in two ways, as explained in 2 Corinthians 5:21. The first has to do with sin. The writer to the Hebrews wrote, "For we do not have a high priest who cannot sympathize with our weaknesses, but One who has been tempted in all things as we are, yet without sin" (Heb 4:15). Peter the Apostle affirmed this same truth. Speaking of Christ, he wrote, "Who committed no sin, nor was any deceit found in His mouth" (1 Pet 2:22). Paul described Jesus as "Him who knew no sin" (2 Cor 5:21). But our sins were imputed to the sinless account of Christ's life. God performs this imputation. "He made Him . . . to be sin on our behalf" (2 Cor 5:21). Peter explains, "And He Himself bore our sins in His body on the cross" (1 Pet 2:24). This is the dark side of imputation performed at the cross. All the sins of all men of all time were imputed to Christ's account and a just, appropriate sentence executed at the cross.

The other side of imputation is Christ's righteousness put to our account. The answer of Christ to the darkness of our sin is His own perfect righteousness. When God looks at our account, He sees Christ's righteousness imputed or credited to *our account*, "so that we might become the righteousness of God in Him" (2 Cor 5:21). Christ's obedience at the cross undid the sin brought on us all by Adam. Paul explained, "For as through the one man's disobedience the many were made sinners, even so through the obedience of the One the many will be made righteous" (Rom 5:19).

By the work of Christ on the cross, we now stand with a record of righteousness, His righteousness placed to our account. This is called positional righteousness. We are once for all righteous in God's eyes. Our names are written in the Lamb's book of life, never to be removed. We are righteous in Christ.

In addition to this positional righteousness that we enjoy through Christ, we have now been made new, born again by the work of the Holy Spirit performed at our salvation. This is called regeneration. Through regeneration, we have a new, ruling disposition, which is daily strengthened by grace through the ministry of the Holy Spirit, empowering us to live more and more righteously each day. Through faith and obedience motivated by love, we become more conformed to the image of Christ and the commands of Scripture. We think, feel, speak, and do the right things. We live righteously. This is called practical righteousness. With Christ's righteousness imputed to us at salvation, we are accepted in the beloved, part of the household of Faith and can now live righteously for His glory each day. We are now servants of righteousness, not servants of sin.

Prayer

"Lord Jesus, we praise you for altering our record forever. No longer is it a record of sin ending in condemnation eternally. You took our sinful record as your own and paid the just price for all our sins at the cross. In its place, you put your perfect record of complete righteousness to our account. When God our Father looks at our record, He sees your record. We rest in the peace you give because of that fact. Every day is a day of joy as we consider this reality. Even though we struggle to refuse temptation and fail by sinning, requiring confession, our hearts always return to the calming truth of our positional righteousness in you, imputed to us by your great grace. We praise you and exalt you for this amazing grace. Amen."

18

Justification through the Cross

"Much more then, having now been justified by
His blood, we shall be saved from the wrath of
God through Him."
Romans 5:9

Christ shed His blood on the cross that we might be justified. To be justified means to be declared righteous by God on the merits of what Jesus did on the cross. The idea of justification has its roots in the legal setting of a courtroom. God is the Judge and He declares us not guilty for our sins, but eternally in a right standing with Him. Instead of bearing God's wrathful punishment for sin, through Christ we are declared innocent. We are assured that we will never face the Great White Throne judgment (Rev 20:11–15), the time appointed at which those who do not know Christ will be condemned to eternal punishment according to their works. First, whether their name is written in the book of eternal life will be determined. Then, the record of their sins will be considered and just punishment assigned. They will spend forever in the lake of fire. The believer will not face this judgment because of justification.

In our undeserved justification by God as believers, we find a source of daily rejoicing. We are helped by it to respond to the exhortation written by Paul, "Rejoice in the Lord always; again, I will say, rejoice" (Phil 4:4). We stood condemned because of our sins, alienated from God. There certainly is no rejoicing to be found in that. But the path to joy over our justification begins with considering the change that has occurred in our eternal destiny. Once we lived in the fear and dread of facing a God who knows all things about us and is perfect in His assignment of righteous justice. Both our sin nature and the sins we have committed would have made facing such a God utterly terrifying. Living a life anticipating this inevitable appointment with God is the definition of daily misery. But instead, we now face no prospect of this judgment. We only anticipate the kind face and gracious words of Christ at the Bema Seat, who will reward us for what we have done of lasting spiritual value as believers, removing forever every memory of sin and failure.

The way of joy opens even more widely to us daily through our justification. "Therefore, having been justified by faith, we have peace with God through our Lord Jesus Christ" (Rom 5:1). Day by day we enjoy peace in our relationship with God. He views us as objects of His care, strengthening us and guiding us. He sees us as a Father who protects us, nurtures us, and assures us by His Spirit in our hearts. "Therefore there is now no condemnation for those who are in Christ Jesus" (Rom 8:1). "Who will bring a charge against God's elect? God is the one who justifies; who is the one who condemns? Christ Jesus is He who died, yes, rather who was raised, who is at the right hand of God, who also intercedes for us" (Rom 8:34).

Now that the guilt and the punishment for our sins have been paid for on the cross and we have been declared justified by faith, Christ intercedes for us at the right hand of God as our advocate whenever we fail through sinning. "My little children, I am writing these things to you so that you may not sin. And if anyone sins, we have an Advocate with the Father, Jesus Christ the righteous" (1 John 2:1). When the memory of our sins, past and present, and our own hearts rise up to threaten us and bring us low, our Great High Priest triumphantly speaks, "They are forgiven, they are declared righteous through the cross!" "In whatever our heart condemns us; God is greater than our heart and knows all things. Beloved, if our heart does not condemns us we have confidence before God" (1 John 3:20–21).

Prayer

"Our righteous Father, we thank you for your justice, true and unwavering. The Judge of all the earth will always do right! We praise you that your justice required payment for sin, our sins. We were guilty and condemned for sin, and justly so. But, oh Lord, in you are depths of mercy to pour out your justice on your Son for our sins, which He bore for us on the cross. Now we stand in Him, not condemned but declared righteous, justified by His blood. We rest in peace in your tender mercies which are new to us every morning, to us the "declared-just" ones who live in Him who justifies all who trust in Him. Amen."

19

Adoption through the Cross

*"So that He might redeem those who were under
the Law, that we might receive
the adoption of sons."*
Galatians 4:5

At the moment you trusted Christ, your position changed from being a slave under the condemnation of the Law, a slave to sin, and a slave to the fear of death caused by Satan who had the power of death. You became a bondservant or slave of Christ instead. As your new Master, Christ's intent for you was only benevolent in every way, to transform you into His own image. But your change of position for eternity was even further enhanced by receiving adoption into the family of God as an adult son or daughter, not just freedom from being a slave to sin.

The adoption of an adult male to become a son was a legal practice in the first century. At adoption, that son was vested with all the rights and privileges of a biologically born son. These were greater rights than those enjoyed by a minor child in the family, who had not yet reached maturity. These rights included inheritance and responsibilities within the family.

This analogy from first century life reflected in the language of the New Testament helps us understand the privileges we enjoy from the instant of our saving faith in Christ's work for us on the cross. These privileges have always been God's intention for us as believers. Paul explained, "He predestined us to adoption as sons through Jesus Christ to Himself, according to the kind intention of His will" (Eph 1:5). As a son in the family of God, we have the responsibility to obey the Father of the household. His commandments, found in His Word, should not be grievous or burdensome to us, as 1 John 5:3 teaches. Obeying Him is a way to show our love for Him and submission to His will as a responsible member of the family of God. It is evidence that we are in fact a son of God. As John taught, "The one who keeps His commandments abides in Him, and He in him. We know by this that He abides in us by the Spirit whom He has given us" (1 John 5:24).

As an adopted adult son or daughter in the family of God, we enjoy the wealth of the family and an ever-unfolding understanding of those riches as the Spirit opens our eyes when we read the Scriptures. Paul explains, "Now we have received not the spirit of the world, but the Spirit who is from God, so that we may know the things freely given to us by God" (1 Cor 2:12). He wants us to understand "all that God has prepared for those who love Him" (1 Cor 2:10).

Our inheritance in Christ as an adult son in the family of God continues beyond this life. He has "raised us up with Him, and seated us with Him in the heavenly places in Christ Jesus, so that in the ages to come He might show the surpassing riches of His grace in kindness toward us in Christ Jesus" (Eph 2:6–7). We have "an inheritance which is imperishable and undefiled and will not fade away, reserved in heaven for" us (1 Peter 1:4).

This life is of immeasurable importance. In it we are to serve Him faithfully for His glory by spreading the gospel, building up the Church, and growing in the image of Christ. But our service will not end here in this world. "His bond-servants will serve Him" in the New Heaven, the New Earth, and the New Jerusalem (Rev 22:3) and enjoy an inheritance as prince-priests beyond all imagination. We will do this in transformed bodies, a gift because of our adoption, as we begin eternity with Him (Rom 8:23). This is our destiny.

Prayer

"Father, thank you for making us your sons and daughters by adoption through Christ's work on the cross. We are overwhelmed with the privilege we experience in this life and will experience in the next because of it. Give us grace to faithfully obey as your sons and daughters today. When others meet us, may they see your glory. When others speak with us, may they hear your voice. When others receive our help, may they know your compassionate heart. Help us as sons and daughters of God to be like you. Create in us a hunger and thirst for your Word as we seek out the riches you have prepared for us now because you love us. Help us set our affections on things above, where moth and rust do not corrupt, where you have laid up treasures for us in Heaven. In the name of your Son we pray. Amen."

20

Reconciliation through the Cross

*"For if while we were enemies we were reconciled
to God through the death of His Son, much more,
having been reconciled, we shall
be saved by His life."*
Romans 5:10

Who are the enemies of God? Some are not difficult to identify. Atheists who deny His existence are His enemies. Agnostics who acknowledge that God may exist but view Him as uninterested in and irrelevant to daily life are adversaries of God. Men who oppose the teaching of Scripture and advance falsehood oppose Him and His Truth. These all follow the way of their unseen and often unacknowledged leader, Satan. They are the enemies of God.

Are there any other enemies of God in the world? What about those who never aggressively oppose God? There are hundreds of millions of men and women who are not Christians, who work day in and day out to prosper in this world, never thinking an antagonistic thought about God. Often, they have no thoughts of God at all. They are godless. Are they the enemies of God?

There is no ambiguity in Scripture about who the enemies of God are. Paul wrote, "And you were dead in your trespasses and sins, in which you formerly walked according to the course of this world, according to the prince of the power of the air, of the spirit that is now working in the sons of disobedience" (Eph 2:1–2). All those who do not know Christ are "the sons of disobedience" and live a life that opposes God. They are the enemies of God. Most men and women without Christ do not view themselves this way. If asked whether they oppose God in any way, they would likely say, "I have nothing against God at all. If people want to believe in Him and follow His way, that's fine with me. That's just not the way I prefer to live." And therein lies the problem. They are living in darkness about the reality of their condition and their position in opposition to God—they are in fact His enemies and don't even realize it. That is a dangerous position to be in. The God who created them, sustains them in life, and sent His Son to redeem them from sin is the One they oppose, often by simply ignoring Him.

God, abounding in mercy, knows the danger men are in without Christ. He therefore instructs believers, "Therefore, we are ambassadors for Christ, as though God were making an appeal through us; we beg you on behalf of Christ, be reconciled to God. He made Him who knew no sin to be sin on our behalf, so that we might be made the righteousness of God in Him" (2 Cor 5:20–21). This war between God and men and women everywhere can be stopped and a permanent peace treaty signed between them because of what Christ did on the cross. He became sin for all lost persons, bore their penalty for sin, and provides a righteous standing before God for them. The God who has been their enemy will become their Friend, their Father, and their King if they place faith in Christ's sacrifice for them on the cross.

As soldiers in God's army, believers must never be traitorous or inactive in the war for the spread of righteousness and truth. As the Apostle Paul urged, "Put on the full armor of God, so that you will be able to stand firm against the schemes of the devil . . . . Therefore, take up the full armor of God, so that you will be able to resist in the evil day, and having done everything, to stand firm" (Eph 6:11, 13). Our aim is to remain in harmony with our Leader, fully reconciled to His purposes. But we are also ambassadors bringing others to that place of reconciliation with Him, so that the war between every man and God may cease through faith in His reconciling work on the cross.

Prayer

"Lord, thank you that through your Son we may live in complete harmony with you forever. Where there was war between us, there now is peace. We praise you that you made us your servants who were once your enemies. We are reconciled with you. Your ways are now our ways, and your purposes are now our purposes. Your hopes for others are now our hopes, that they may surrender to you, enter into your peace through Christ's work on the cross, and be reconciled fully to your will as God. May it be so, Lord, may it be so. Amen."

21

Words of Forgiveness from the Cross

"Father, forgive them; for they know
not what they do."
Luke 23:34

While Jesus hung on the Cross, He spoke. Seven of His statements from the Cross are recorded in the Gospels. These are the last of His words to be heard by man before His death for the sins of men. They were spoken from the crucible of intense suffering, suffering such as no one else has ever suffered before, or since. The first statement was "Father, forgive them; for they know not what they do." That His first words from the cross were ones of forgiveness is significant. Forgiveness for sin is the heart, the very intention of Christ's work on the cross.

This statement is a prayer to His Father in Heaven. Christ was keenly aware that the unjust trials, the vicious beatings, the heartless mockery and the savage crucifixion were sins of the darkest kind. He begged His Father to forgive those responsible.

They were guilty to varying degrees because of their varying knowledge. None of them understood the full depth of the crime they were committing. Jesus asked His Father to forgive them "for they know not what they do." What were they doing? Murdering the God of Life, their Creator, their Redeemer, the Son of God who came to save them! No crime has ever been committed like this one, before or since.

Worst and most responsible were the Jewish leaders who plotted His death out of envy and their lust for power and wealth. Next were Pilate and Herod, political figures who allowed themselves to be manipulated to perform this "legal" murder out of self-interest. Then there were the soldiers who mocked Christ, beat Him, gambled for His clothes, and performed the crucifixion in "the line of duty." The crowds participated by calling for His death at the provocation of their religious leaders and mocking Him while He hung on the Cross. Feasting on the bloody thrill of the moment, enjoying the satisfying of their morbid curiosity, they watched Jesus suffer and be killed.

For these Jesus prayed for forgiveness. If ever there was a model of the depth and scope of what forgiveness means, it is this. Despite their bitter hatred and casual indifference to His suffering, He asked His Father to cancel out their sin, to erase it from the divine record. None of the perpetrators of these crimes asked for this forgiveness, but Christ pled for it.

From these words of Jesus, we learn that our greatest efforts for the redemption of men may be mocked, our efforts spurned. Christ suffered while seeking no revenge, but rather sought forgiveness for those who opposed Him resulting in His death. In these words of forgiveness that Jesus prayed, we learn the importance of the spiritual destiny of men over our own physical destiny. Jesus was suffering in agony, He was dying, but He was praying for the relationship of His enemies with God, not His own physical deliverance.

We learn, too, of Christ's endurance in the mission God had given Him. No sin of man against Him would deter Him from the act that would serve as the fountainhead of forgiveness for all men, for all time. Jesus "for the joy set before Him endured the cross, despising the shame, and sat down at the right hand of the throne of God. For consider Him who has endured such hostility by sinners against Himself, so that you will not grow weary and lose heart" (Heb 12:2b–3).

Prayer

"Lord, give us hearts that forgive those who sin against us. Help us pray for lost men who despise us and despise the gospel. Give us patience to pray for forgiveness for those who sin against you repeatedly, who ask no forgiveness but need it desperately. Give us eyes to see beyond our physical needs and desires to the spiritual condition of those around us who need your forgiveness. Help us bring the blessing of forgiveness to all we know through the good news of the cross by faithfully proclaiming it to everyone we know. This we pray in the name of the Lord Jesus. Amen."

22

Words for the Lost from the Cross

"And He said to him, Truly I say to you, today you shall be with Me in Paradise."
Luke 23:43

Two criminals were crucified with Christ. One hung on a cross to Christ's right and the other on His left. Luke 23:39–43 gives an account of the striking contrast between the two of them in their response to their circumstances and to Jesus. In these two men and Christ's response to one of them, we witness the great divide between all men in their response to Christ as the Savior. This is Christ's second statement from the cross after His statement of forgiveness.

One of the criminals He was crucified with was railing on Jesus, bitterly mocking Him by saying, "'Are You not the Christ? Save Yourself and us!'" (Luke 23:39). The rebuke given him by the other criminal, hanging on his own cross, captures the true spirit in which this angry, desperate man uttered his caustic words. "But the other answered, and rebuking him said, 'Do you not even fear God, since you are under the same sentence of condemnation? And we indeed are suffering justly, for we are receiving what we deserve for our deeds; but this man has done nothing wrong'" (vv. 40–41).

There was no fear of God in this man's failed attempt to shame Jesus into performing a miracle for all three of them, and there certainly was no honesty in it. He was guilty of the crime for which he was being executed and he had no real saving faith in Jesus. Though his guilt is clear, and the end of his life is imminent, he refuses to see past this life and to see the deliverance from sin and final judgment he could experience through Christ. This man's life stands forever as a profound example of the irrationality of sin and the blindness of the lost, even when faced with death. For the believer this is a motivation to get the truth of the gospel to the lost often and early, before the duress of suffering in their final hours distorts their judgment. Men may remain in spiritual blindness in their last hour of life, beyond all hope.

Hanging on a cross in the worst circumstances imaginable, the other criminal at the hour of his death said of Jesus, ". . . but this man has done nothing wrong" (v. 41b), even though he had been mocking Christ earlier along with the other criminal being crucified with Christ. He acknowledged the innocence of Jesus, both with reference to any crime for which He was charged and for His behavior while suffering crucifixion. The criminal had already acknowledged his own guilt. In one short statement, he expressed his saving faith in Christ: "'Jesus, remember me when You come into Your kingdom'" (v. 42). His words reveal that He understood Jesus was the King of the eternal kingdom, not a physical realm. He trusted Jesus for entrance into that kingdom. His words indicate that he had understanding about the saving mission of the Messiah. At the moment in his life when there was nothing he could do to save himself, no good works he could perform, and no religious ritual he could engage in, he believed. His faith was of such a quality that Jesus responded, "'Truly I say to you, today you shall be with Me in Paradise" (v. 43).

Christ's promise to this man is astonishing. He promised the man that he would be with Him in paradise that day, meaning at the man's death. The word paradise is one of the terms for Heaven in the New Testament, where there is comfort, peace, service, and the presence of God forever. These words of Jesus to this man teach us that men may be saved up until their last moment of life. As believers, we must never give up in our attempts to reach them. These words of Jesus also reveal that even an entire life invested wrongly can anticipate the glories and benefits of Heaven by faith in Christ alone as Savior. Eternal salvation is by God's grace alone.

Prayer

"Oh, dear Son of God, we praise you for your compassion for the lost. While bearing the sin of the whole world on the cross and in complete physical agony, you were burdened for the two lost men hanging on either side of you. Even when viciously mocked by them, you gave no harsh rebuke. To your last hours you lived with a vision for what men could become by faith in you. You labored for them to turn from sin to you as Savior, the Great Shepherd of all lost sheep. We magnify and glorify you, the Good Shepherd, who saves us and guides us to your Heavenly Kingdom. Amen."

23

Words for His Family from the Cross

"Woman, behold, your son!
. . . Behold, your mother!"
John 19:26–27

Jesus was the oldest son in a large family. The record of the Gospels indicates that His mother was a widow. There is no appearance of Joseph, His father, after His early life at age 12 (Luke 2:41–52), when He visited the Temple with His mother and father. He had four brothers (James, Joses, Judas, and Simon, Mark 6:3)) and at least two sisters (also mentioned though unnamed, Mark 6:3). In His role as the oldest son, He bore special responsibility for the care of His widowed mother.

In more than one episode in the Gospels, there is indication that His brothers were not yet believers during some of His public ministry. They taunted Him on one occasion about going into Judea from Galilee to celebrate the Feast of Booths to reveal Himself to the people more widely. They said, "'For no one does anything in secret when he himself seeks to be known publicly. If you do these things, show yourself to the world.' For not even His brothers were believing in Him" (John 7:5). Later, at least two of His brothers did become devoted believers: James, who became the leader of the elders of the church in Jerusalem, and Jude, the author of the epistle bearing his name in the New Testament.

At one point early in His ministry, His family members thought that He had become mentally imbalanced because of His constant efforts in His work of healing and preaching. Mark records, "And He came home, and the crowd gathered again to such an extent that they could not even eat a meal. When His own people heard of this, they went out to take custody of Him; for they were saying, 'He has lost His senses'" (Mark 3:20–21). Standing outside, they sent word into His house in Capernaum where He was healing and teaching. The crowd sitting around Him told Him they were calling for Him. Jesus answered them by saying, 'Who are My mother and My brothers?' Looking about at those who were sitting around Him, He said, 'Behold My mother and My brothers! For whoever does the will of God, he is My brother and sister and mother'" (Mark 3:33–35). In these statements, Jesus establishes a hierarchy in relationships. Obedient believers who do the will of God are those with whom the Christian will experience the closest fellowship and most common purpose. These relationships may be even more intimate than the natural bonds of human family.

Jesus taught directly about the responsibility of children to their parents, especially to honor and to care for them in older age, affirming the teaching of the ten commandments (Exod 20:12; Mark 7:9–10). He strongly refuted the teaching of the Pharisees which said that if a man had dedicated his wealth to God he had no responsibility to care for elderly parents (Mark 7:11–13). Paul later affirms Christ's teaching on this subject in Ephesians 6:1–3, "Children, obey your parents in the Lord, for this is right. Honor your father and mother (which is the first commandment with a promise), so that it may be well with you, and that you may live long on the earth" (quoting Exod 20:12 and Deut 5:16).

The Lord Jesus considered His responsibility for His mother, a believer, so important that while He was dying on the cross, He assigned the care of His mother after His death to John the Apostle. "Then He said to the disciple, 'Behold, your mother!' From that hour the disciple took her into his own household" (John 19:26–27). Just before that He addressed His mother about her new relationship with John. "When Jesus then saw His mother, and the disciple whom He loved standing nearby, He said to His mother, 'Woman, behold, your son!" (John 19:26). She needed to see John, not her biological sons, as the son that would care for her after Jesus' death.

Christ's deep confidence in John the Apostle caused Jesus to assign the care of His widowed mother to a godly non-family friend whom He trusted. In doing this, the Lord Jesus demonstrated the great care to be given to the spiritual welfare of our older parents, not only their familial, social, and physical care. He handed His "eldest son" responsibilities over to a godly man He trusted, with a trust that transcended family ties.

Prayer

"Father, how we thank you for our families, our flesh and blood. We resolve, Lord, to seek their salvation and growth spiritually. We resolve to obey you by the care we give to our parents when they reach older age. Thank you for the promise of blessing on us if we obey this commandment, cited both in your Law and repeated in the New Testament. Give us wisdom and compassion for the spiritual well-being of our parents in older age, not just their physical well-being. And Lord Jesus, thank you for our spiritual brothers and sisters to whom we may turn for care of our parents if needed. We glorify you for your example of care for your mother in the closing hours of your life. Amen."

24

Words of Broken Fellowship from the Cross

"My God, My God, why have You forsaken Me?"
Matthew 27:46

Before Adam and Eve chose to sin in Eden, they enjoyed perfect communion with God. Their relationship with Him was the essence of life for them. God came to them in the garden, blessing them with His presence and His care. This harmonious relationship with God, the creature with the Creator, was how life was meant be in this world. It was a life of unity with God and all the attendant blessings as a result.

However, succumbing to the temptation of the Evil One, who came in the form of a serpent, brought fear and disharmony in their relationship with God. Adam and Eve hid in the garden from God. They forsook God through their disobedience. He had to pursue them, find them, and bring them back into a right relationship with Him. God took the initiative to restore harmony with them.

Now, because of the sin of Adam, every man, woman, and child comes into this world separated from God, forsaken of Him. There is only one remedy for this. It is the initiative God took through His Son, Jesus Christ. He had to become our sin-bearer and He suffered the punishment for us for those sins. "He made Him who knew no sin to be sin on our behalf, so that we might become the righteousness of God in Him" (2 Cor 5:21). As Peter further explains, "And He Himself bore our sins in His body on the cross, so that we might die to sin and live to righteousness; for by His wounds you were healed" (1 Pet 2:24).

At its heart, sin is selfish, prideful rebellion against God, a choosing to go one's own way. Living a life independent of God is the ambition of those lost in sin. Separation from God is the desired state. To be alienated from God, apart from Him is to live a life of no obligation to Him, no responsibility to obey His laws or to seek a relationship with Him. What the person without Christ seeks, this separateness from God, is the heart of the problem God has addressed through the cross.

Christ bore all this rebellion and alienation from God in Himself on the cross. He bore all this sin of man and therefore experienced what only He could experience as the God-Man—a limitless, hopeless darkness away from God the Father. Being alienated or forsaken by God was not only *the result* of the sin He bore for us. It was *the very soul* of our sin--our rebellious alienation from God. After three hours of darkness that fell on the earth from 12:00 noon to approximately 3:00 pm, Jesus quoted Psalm 22:1, "My God, My God, why have You forsaken me?" There is a depth of mystery in how God the Son could be so utterly alienated from God the Father. For the perfect communion in the Trinity to be disrupted by sin is a spiritual agony we cannot comprehend.

Analogies drawn from life give us some glimpse of what this "forsakenness" was like. How does a child feel when his father abandons him and his family, and never returns? What does a wife feel when her husband of many years leaves her for someone else? To be permanently forsaken is devastating beyond description. Christ bore that abandonment for us so that we may abide in Christ day by day and forever. In place of the sadness of being forsaken, God says, "I will never desert you, nor will I ever forsake you" (Heb 13:5).

Prayer

"Lord Jesus, thank you that through the cross you freed us from being alone, abandoned by God. You were separated from the perfect communion with the Father for us. You plummeted to a depth of darkness in sin, alone and apart from all that is good. By your work on the cross you assure us that we will never be forsaken by you, the Father, and the Holy Spirit. We may ever live in communion with you, knowing the warmth of your presence, the constant cleansing of your blood, the ever in-flowing of your love. By your abiding presence, we know your strengthening in the inner man and your assurance that we are sons and daughters of God. Thank you for never forsaking us day by day, and forever. Amen."

25

Words of Agony
from the Cross

"I thirst."
John 19:28

Christ was offered sour wine to drink twice while He was on the cross. First, He was offered sour wine (a light, water-diluted wine turned to vinegar) mixed with myrrh. This was done immediately upon arrival at Golgotha, which meant the Place of the Skull. This was a small mercy being offered by the soldiers to address His physical agony. It was offered before He was nailed to the cross, the climax of the torture He had been enduring. He had already been scourged, leaving his back a bloody mass of flesh and muscle. The pain being endured already by Christ was horrific. Then they tried to give Him wine mixed with myrrh; but He did not take it" (Mark 15:23). Matthew 27:34 says that the wine was mixed with "gall," which is a word for any bitter substance, such as myrrh.

Myrrh was a resinous gum from a bush grown in the Arabian Peninsula. When mixed with wine, the effect would be to kill the pain and lessen the suffering of the one being crucified, not primarily to quench his thirst. When Christ tasted this light wine (the normal beverage of the soldiers, though now sour) mixed with myrrh, He refused to drink it because He knew what the effect would be. Escaping the physical suffering of the cross was not the aim of Christ. He intended to suffer to the fullest measure for our sins, not have the pain deadened by a chemical substance.

Just before His death, after crying out "My God, My God, why have You forsaken Me?" (Matt 27:46) and commending his mother to the care of John, Jesus said, "I am thirsty" (John 19:28). "A jar full of sour wine was standing there; so they put a sponge full of the sour wine upon a branch of hyssop and brought it up to His mouth" (John 19:29). There was no myrrh to deaden pain in this sour wine. He had endured the hours of scourging and crucifixion now. He was at the end, suffering the debilitating effects of dehydration, all part of the agony of the death He was dying for us.

The offering of two drinks to Christ on the Cross underscores the agony Christ was suffering physically in His body for our sins. The death of Christ was a spiritual transaction with eternal consequences, but it was also a physical death of great suffering for every man. He bled real blood. He poured water out as perspiration from every pore of His beaten body. He was bruised, torn, and pierced. He was wounded physically. "But we do see Him who was made for a little while lower than the angels, namely, Jesus, because of the suffering of death crowned with glory and honor, so that by the grace of God He might taste death for everyone" (Heb 2:9). His physical death for us achieved the redemption of our bodies, which will one day be raised incorruptible. As Isaiah 53:5 says, "But He was pierced through for our transgressions, He was crushed for our iniquities; the chastening of our well-being fell upon Him, and by His scourging we are healed." His cry for something to drink allowed Him to declare clearly, "It is finished!" (John 19:30). The work of redemption was done.

Prayer

"Lord Jesus, the thought of what you bore on the cross for us causes us to weep with sorrow and weep with joy. What agony you endured for us! And what healing you achieved for us through your death! By your stripes we are healed, spiritually. Someday physically we will stand before you in resurrected bodies redeemed by your physical suffering on the cross. Your example compels us to endure any physical suffering that we may face as we serve you. You "who for the joy set before [you] endured the cross, despising the shame, and have sat down at the right hand of the throne of God" for us (Heb 12:2). Your thirst on the cross was physical. But there was another thirst that was only quenched by doing the will of your Father. Cause our thirst for performing your will to increase until it is fully satisfied by obedience and we finally awake in your likeness. In your name, our Savior and our God, we pray. Amen."

26

Words of Triumph
from the Cross

"It is finished!"
John 19:30

"But when the fullness of time came, God sent forth His Son, born of a woman, born under the Law, so that He might redeem those who were under the Law, that we might receive the adoption of sons" (Gal 4:4–5). In this single statement, Paul summarizes the task which Christ came to perform under commission from His Father. He lived a life in perfect conformity to the Law, and He died a perfect death to redeem mankind and offer salvation to all who would believe. Nothing remains to be done for the salvation of any man who believes in the death, burial, and resurrection of Jesus.

This is a great distinction between biblical Christianity and Christianity in its many false forms, as well as the other false religions of the world. Christianity in its many false forms requires more than faith in the death and resurrection of Christ for salvation. There must be the keeping of special laws and sacraments of those false forms of Christianity and the performing of good works prescribed. There must be a belief in special prophecies in addition to the Bible or in contradiction to the Bible. There must be a faith in the founder of that religion as a special messenger from God, a founder whose message is usually believed superior to the prophecies in the Scriptures.

In contrast to the false forms of Christianity and other false religions in the world, when Jesus cried out, "It is finished!" what did He mean? He meant that all the predictive prophecies in the Old Testament about His death had been fulfilled. He meant that all the laws of the Old Testament had been obeyed to the fullest extent. He meant that all the symbolic ceremonial worship system of the Old Testament became reality through His death. He meant that he who had the power of death, Satan, was defeated. He meant that by faith men could now come to know freedom from the law of sin. He meant that the way of peace with God had been made open. He meant that men could be declared righteous by faith in His death. He meant that all the wrath of God for sin had been borne to God's complete satisfaction. He meant that His righteousness could now be put to the account of all who believe in Him. He meant that all those who believe will live again in new bodies purchased by His blood. He meant that His incarnate work was complete, allowing for His ascension to assume His role as the High Priest of Heaven with an ongoing intercessory ministry at the right hand of God for us. He meant that now He and the Father could send the Spirit to dwell in the hearts of believers to make them sons of God. He meant that the Cornerstone of the Church had been laid. He meant that the King of Kings and Lord of Lords, the Lion-Lamb of Judah was victorious and will reign in His kingdom forever.

There is yet another sense in which "It is finished" should be understood. Christ's love of the Father made the fulfillment of His will paramount in the mind of Christ. In the Garden of Gethsemane, Christ prayed that if the Father would allow Him not to go through the experience of the cross, He would be grateful for it due to the horrific nature of the sacrifice. But He always added that He wanted the Father's will, not His own. The Father's will for the incarnation was complete—it was finished. Christ endured the cross for us. By so doing He followed the Father's will.

Prayer

"Father, your will for Christ was fulfilled. He died for our sins. Your wisdom in the way of the cross is past finding out. It is the eternal payment to satisfy perfect justice and demonstrate your perfect love. Lord Jesus, thank you for finishing your work on the cross for us. Thank you for the five bleeding wounds you bore, the scourging, the mockery, the beatings, and the thorns. Most of all, thank you for loving us with a greater love than any man could by giving your life for us. We glorify you! We magnify you! We rejoice in you! Amen."

27

Words of Victorious Submission from the Cross

"Father, into Your hands I commend My spirit."
Luke 23:46

Like His first statement from the cross, Christ's seventh and last statement was a prayer. The first was a prayer to His heavenly Father for forgiveness for those responsible for His death. This prayer, also to His Father, was one of victorious submission to the Father's care at the hour of His death. Three times in the Garden of Gethsemane, Christ had prayed the same prayer: "My Father, if it is possible, let this cup pass from Me; yet not as I will, but as You will (Matthew 26:39). This had been true of Christ during the whole time He was the God-man. He was submitted to His Father's will, to obey it explicitly and fully. As God the Son in eternity, He had always been in an intimate relationship with God the Father. But when He was conceived by the influence of the God the Spirit over Mary, He became "the Son of God" (Luke 1:35) also in the sense of submission to the Father's will and His plan of redemption for fallen man.

Through His final prayer, Christ models how we should die. He had just cried out in victory, "It is finished!" He had accomplished in fullest measure man's salvation from sin. His work was done. He had done the Father's will, living a righteous life and dying a redeeming death for the sins of man. It was the hour of His death now, and He would continue as He had throughout His life, trusting the care of His spirit to the Father, anticipating His resurrection and return to Heaven and His divine glory. We must trust our Father at moment of our death, as Christ did. The glories of our redeemed bodies, our rewards, Heaven, and most of all His presence await us. We shall be like Him, for we shall see Him as He is!

Through His final prayer, our Master also demonstrated that He was God, controlling all the events at the Cross, even the very moment of His death. Earlier in His ministry He had taught concerning His life, "No one has taken it away from Me, because I lay down My life so that I may take it again. No one has taken it from Me, but I lay it down on My own initiative. I have authority to lay it down, and I have authority to take it up again. This commandment I received from the Father" (John 10:18). All the scheming of the Jewish leaders merely performed His will as He fulfilled the Father's will. When Pilate, in frustration over Christ's reluctance to answer his questions, said he had the power to release Him or take Christ's life, Jesus said, "You would have no authority over Me, unless it had been given you from above; for this reason he who delivered Me to you has the greater sin" (John 19:10).

Christ's sovereign control over His life and His death was demonstrated by His deciding when He would die. After saying, "Into Your hands I commend My spirit," the Scriptures say, "Having said this, He breathed His last" (Luke 23:46), which literally means He dismissed His spirit as an act of His own will, precisely fulfilling what He had told the Pharisees earlier in His ministry He would do (John 10:18).

The will of the Father determined all that Christ would suffer, the nature of His death, down to the detail, including the duration of His time on the Cross, which was approximately six hours (9:00 a.m. to 3:00 p.m.). Death by crucifixion usually took at least a whole day, but historical records give accounts of men suffering up to nine days on the cross. The intensity of Christ's suffering, the full wrath of God, made it possible to accomplish what was necessary in just six hours. Sometimes what occurs briefly on one day can shape the destiny of a man's life, a nation, and even the whole world. That was true concerning the death of Christ.

The Father and the Son planned and executed redemption for us, down to the details. Their concern for us extends to every detail of our lives, down to the number of hairs on our head. We can rest in the care of our God, who is abundant in lovingkindness, gracious, slow to anger, and full of compassion. As Paul wrote, "He who did not spare His own Son, but delivered Him over for us all, how will He not freely give us all things?" (Rom 8:31).

Prayer

"Father, we lift our hearts in praise to you for our redemption, planned with and achieved through the Son. By your Spirit, give us the same submission for the completion of your will in our lives that Christ demonstrated in His, to the moment of His death. Forgive us for not resting in your sovereign control of all things that concern us, the sovereign control that Christ demonstrated at the cross. We rejoice in your promise that the death of Christ is our assurance of your never-ending provision and care by your grace for all of life, proven by rescuing us from sin and hell. With thanks and joy we pray. Amen."

28

The Cross for
All the World

*"For it is for this we labor and strive,
because we have fixed our hope on the living God,
who is the Savior of all men, especially of believers."*
1 Timothy 4:10

As disciples of Jesus, we are to labor to the point of exhaustion, straining with all our energy to live a life of godliness fixed in hope on the living God. Christ is the living God, risen from His death on the cross for our sins. Christ is our Savior because we have personally exercised saving repentance and faith in His death and resurrection. Enabled through this trust to turn from sin to Christ, we have forgiveness of sins and the gift of eternal life. He is "the Savior of all men, especially of believers." In this blessed reality we find great encouragement because we are believers.

There is also great encouragement and motivation found in the fact that the Lord Jesus, who is God, is "the Savior of *all* men," as 1 Tim 4:10 says (italics added). In what ways is this true? First it is true that Christ's death on the Cross was sufficient payment for the redemption of every living person on earth, the nearly eight billion of them that inhabit this globe and all those who have lived before, as well as those who will live in the future. His "precious blood" shed in death, which was more valuable than all silver and gold, was the price paid, according 1 Peter 1:19. God so loved the whole world that He gave His only begotten Son for them that they might believe and receive everlasting life, as John 3:16 teaches.

Second, John the Apostle also wrote, "He himself is the propitiation for our sins; and not ours only, but also for those of *the whole world*" (1 John 2:2, italics added). Propitiation means that Christ bore all the just wrath of God for all the sins of all men on the cross, and by this God's justice is satisfied.

Third, "God was in Christ reconciling *the world* unto Himself, not counting their trespasses against them, and He has committed to us the word of reconciliation" (2 Cor 5:19, italics added). What God did through His son on the

Cross was enough to bring permanent peace between every man and his Creator.

The redemption, propitiation, and reconciliation accomplished by Christ for every person must be claimed by each of them through faith in Him. Unless a person exercises saving faith in Jesus, His death—though more than sufficient for anyone's salvation—will not result in salvation for that person. Each person must apply it to himself individually and personally, as the Spirit of God draws him to Christ and opens his eyes to understand the truth of the gospel.

God wants every man, woman, and child to be saved. As 1 Tim 2:3–4 says, "This is good and acceptable in the sight of God our Savior, who desires *all men* to be saved and to come to the knowledge of the truth" (italics added). "The Lord is not slow about His promise, as some count slowness, but is patient toward you, not wishing for any to perish but for *all to come to repentance*" (2 Pet 3:9, italics added). Christ's death was for the whole world of sinful people, and it is God's desire that they all be saved. Our hearts must align with God's heart in this. This truth should motivate us to take the good news of salvation to everyone we know and help others go to the ends of the earth to every tongue, tribe, and nation to do the same.

Prayer

"Dear Father, give us a heart like yours for men who are lost in their sin. You sent the Lord Jesus to die for every one of them. He did all that needed to be done to accomplish their salvation through His death. Give us grace to take the message of the cross to all we know so that the Spirit of Christ "will draw all men" to Him (John 12:32). We know that through the incarnation of your Son the saving grace that brings salvation to all has appeared (Titus 2:11). May that saving grace appear to others through us as we live and speak the Truth for your glory. Send laborers into the harvest to reap the lost for your glory, we pray. Amen."

29

Fruitfulness through the Cross

"Truly, truly, I say to you, unless a grain of wheat falls into the earth and dies, it remains alone; but if it dies, it bears much fruit."
John 12:24

During the week leading up to His Cross, after the triumphal entry into Jerusalem, Jesus said, "The hour has come for the Son of Man to be glorified" (John 12:23). He would be glorified by the effect of the power of His death and resurrection. He followed this statement about His glorification by a brief analogy in John 12:24: "Truly, truly, I say to you, unless a grain of wheat falls into the earth and dies, it remains alone, but if it dies, it bears much fruit." Through this analogy about wheat, Christ taught the importance of His death for the future harvest of men's souls. Just as a grain of wheat falls into the soil, is buried, and germinates producing a new harvest, so Christ's death brings the prospect of spiritual life to men. Through His death for sin comes life for all who trust Him by faith.

Immediately after these words concerning His own death and the consequent harvest of life from it, Jesus extended this teaching concerning Himself to His prospective future disciples. He said, "He who loves his life loses it, and he who hates his life in this world will keep it to life eternal" (John 12:25). Every person must come to the moment when he or she determines to "die" to this world and the temporal benefits it offers. This is repentance, a change of thinking and feeling about life without God, resulting in the choice to reject that self-centered life. Only then may one by faith receive the gift of eternal life, as the seed of the message of Christ crucified is received into his heart. A life lived from an eternal perspective, bearing spiritual fruit during this life, will be the result. As Jesus prayed in His high priestly prayer in John 17:3, "This is eternal life, that they may know You, the only true God, and Jesus Christ whom You have sent."

The spiritual harvest in this life may be abundant, as Jesus described in Matt 13:23: "And the one on whom seed was sown on the good soil, this is the man who hears the word and understands it; who indeed bears fruit and brings forth, some a hundredfold, some sixty, and some thirty." Beyond this life, the one who has received the gospel, the message of the cross, will enjoy life forever with God in service to Him. Describing eternity with God, John wrote, "There will no longer be any curse; and the throne of God and the Lamb will be in it, and His bond-servants will serve Him" (Rev 22:3).

Christ then taught even more fully about this life of discipleship beyond saving faith. "If anyone serves Me, he must follow Me; and where I am, there My servant will be also; if anyone serves Me, the Father will honor him" (John 12:26). This service of the disciple of Christ begins with following Him by denying oneself and taking up his own cross (Luke 9:23). All spiritual good through a disciple's life begins with following the supreme example of Jesus in His death on the cross and then following wherever Jesus leads him in service. As Jesus said, "And where I am, there My servant will be also" (John 12:26).

The disciple who desires to bear fruit must always be with Christ. After the last Passover meal with the disciples and on the way to the Garden Gethsemane, Jesus taught His disciples the parable of the vine (John 15:1–17). In it He repeatedly urged His disciples to "abide" with Him. He said in a summative statement, "If you abide in Me, and My words abide in you, ask whatever you wish, and it will be done for you. My Father is glorified by this, that you bear much fruit and so prove to be My disciples" (John 15:7–8). Just like an abundant wheat harvest through receiving the Word of the gospel (the parable of the sower), so we as branches of the Vine, Christ, may bear a great harvest of fruit by faithfully remaining in fellowship with Him through deep pruning from God. This is the removal of all encumbrances to growth. To this must be added loving obedience to His commandments and faith-filled prayer requesting abundant fruitfulness. The disciple who follows Christ in the way of the cross will abound in fruit and "the Father will honor him" (John 12:26), sometimes in this life but always in eternity, where he will receive great reward.

Prayer

"Father, we know from your Word that you want us to abound in fruitfulness for your glory. Just as Jesus suffered death resulting in a great harvest of men and women for eternity, help us embrace death to our selfish ambitions, sinful desires, and the world that seeks to crush us into its mold, so that we may bear an abundant harvest spiritually for you. Give us grace daily to take up our cross and walk in newness of life by your Spirit and the strength He gives. We praise you for your great and precious promises through which we may experience this today for the good of others and for your glory. May your will be done for your glory through us, we pray. Amen."

30

The Priority of Proclaiming the Cross

"But we preach Christ crucified, to Jews a stumbling block and to Gentiles foolishness, but to those who are the called, both Jews and Greeks, Christ the power of God and the wisdom of God."
1 Corinthians 1:23–24

When the saving work of Christ was preached in the first century, there were two responses—rejection of it and acceptance of it by faith for salvation. The twenty-first century mirrors the first in this fact, as has every century since the death, burial, and resurrection of Jesus. Some Jews viewed the good news of the cross as something scandalous, an obstacle in the way of their thinking about God. They stumbled over the idea that Jesus was God since He was man. Though the Old Testament made clear that the Messiah, who was God, would enter the world as a man and die for their sins, they rejected that message out of ignorance (e.g., Is 53:1–12). Their hearts were hardened from their fixation on God as the transcendent Spirit, who (they thought) would never take on a body to live among men and suffer a criminal's death.

On the other hand, some non-Jews who heard the message of the cross, called Gentiles and Greeks in 1 Corinthians 1:23–24, refused the message of the cross because it required trust in the sacrificial death of Christ for sin, the One revealed as the Deliverer. This message rejected all human philosophies of how to live the good life through knowledge, intellectual attainment, and reasoning, in short, the wisdom of this world. Gentiles struggled with this. They still do today. Understanding these responses of rejection should strengthen our faith in Christ. In the parable of the sower, the Lord Jesus foretold that some would accept the message of the cross and some would not (Matt 13:18–23.) The hearts of men are like different kinds of soil. The seed of the gospel produces life and fruit in some and no life and no fruit in others.

Our hope should be fixed on the truth that many will respond to the saving message of the cross. We must not be controlled and fearful because some will reject the message. The fact that there are many who will receive it must compel us to proclaim the gospel of the grace of God through the death and resurrection of Christ. As the Apostle wrote in 1 Cor 1:24, "but to those who are called, both Jews and Greeks, Christ the power of God and the wisdom of God." God sends out His call for all men to be saved through faith in Christ's work on the cross. Those who receive the message by faith are transformed by its power and understand the supreme wisdom of God's redemptive plan as their only hope.

For believers, the Scriptures are full of instruction about the good we should do to our neighbors and to fellow Christians. We have been "created in Christ Jesus for good works, which God prepared beforehand so that we would walk in them" (Eph 2:10). In His Sermon on the Mount, Jesus said, "Let your light shine before men in such a way that they may see your good works and glorify your Father who is in heaven" (Matt 5:16). Paul exhorted Titus to teach the disciples in Crete "to be ready for every good deed" (Titus 3:1). James reminds us that "faith, if it has no works, is dead," good works being the primary evidence of true saving faith (James 2:17). But good works for others without the saving message of the cross do not profit them spiritually. The proclamation of the gospel is to be our priority with everyone we meet, supported by our good works.

The proclamation of the saving message of the cross, affirmed and made complete by Christ's resurrection, is our primary means of bringing glory to God in the world and salvation to those in it. Little wonder that Paul wrote, "For I determined to know nothing among you except Jesus Christ, and Him crucified" (1 Cor 2:2). He was only reflecting the final command of the Lord Jesus to us all: "Go therefore and make disciples of all the nations, baptizing them in the name of the Father and the Son and the Holy

Spirit, teaching them to observe all that I commanded you; and lo, I am with you always, even to the end of the age" (Matt 28:19–20).

Prayer

"Father, thank you for sending your Son to die for us on the cross. We praise you for the message of the cross, which is the power of God and wisdom of God to transform sinners into saints, evil men into holy ones who serve you in love by faith. Lord, keep us from timidity and disobedience in carrying the message of the cross to our friends, our family, our neighbors, and the world. Give us determination and courage to proclaim the glory of the cross to the lost, to find them for you and see them brought into your flock, the Great Shepherd of the sheep. For your glory and for the spread of the truth of the cross, we pray. Amen."

31

The Cross, the Burial, and the Resurrection

*"For I delivered to you as of first importance what
I also received, that Christ died for our sins according to the Scriptures, and that He was buried, and
that He was raised on the third day
according to the Scriptures."*
1 Corinthians 15:3–4

For all who believe, the cross of Christ bears personal, eternal significance only because of the resurrection of Christ, evidenced by the empty tomb in which Christ had been buried. The resurrection of Christ completes the good news of the Cross. Our faith is in a risen, living Savior. His resurrection makes final and irrefutable all that was achieved at the cross. Paul wrote in the great resurrection chapter of the New Testament, 1 Corinthians 15, "And if Christ has not been raised, then our preaching is vain, your faith also is vain . . . . And if Christ has not been raised, your faith is worthless; you are still in your sins" (vv. 14, 17). But Paul also wrote, "But now Christ has been raised from the dead, the first fruits of those who are asleep" (1 Cor 15:20). As he taught in Romans 4:25, Christ "was delivered over because of our transgressions and was raised because of our justification." Our being justified, i.e., declared righteous by God and having Christ's righteousness put to our account by His work on the cross, came to completion in the resurrection of Christ.

The simple clause in 1 Cor 15:3–4 that joins Christ death and Christ's resurrection in the text is not insignificant. It underscores both the reality and certainty of Christ's death, and the reality and certainty of His resurrection. The simple clause is "And that He was buried." All four Gospels describe the burial of Christ. Joseph of Arimathea received the body from Pilate for burial upon his courageous request for it. Nicodemus and Joseph, both members of the Sanhedrin and believers in Jesus, bought the clothes for wrapping the dead body of Jesus and purchased a large quantity of the aromatic and preserving spices traditionally used for the procedure. There was a special guard set at the tomb of Jesus. The tomb was officially sealed, giving legal weight to the reality and finality of Christ's death.

The women of Galilee came on the first day of the week after the Sabbath to complete the preparation of His body after His death with more spices. They were stunned to find the great stone at the mouth of the grave rolled away. Two angels appeared to them at the empty tomb and announced that Christ had risen. These angels had so terrified the guards that had been posted at the request of the Jewish leaders, that they lay still as if dead at the sight of the angels. Peter and John learned of Christ's resurrection from the women. They ran to the tomb and were astounded to find the grave clothes still in the tomb, lying in place, with no body in them and the facial cloth removed and rolled up in a different place in the grave. There was only one explanation for this. Jesus had been raised by the power of God right through the grave clothes. Jesus was buried, and He arose!

For forty days Jesus showed Himself alive to His disciples after His resurrection, having left the tomb, never to return. The climax of this unparalleled period was His ascension into Heaven right before the eyes of His disciples in Bethany. These disciples were assured by two angels that appeared saying to them that Christ would come again, just as He had ascended into Heaven. Christ died, He arose, He ascended to the right hand of the Father to intercede for us, and He will return for us in glory to raise dead believers from their graves and catch living Christians up to Heaven through the rapture of the saints.

Prayer

"Lord Jesus, our living Redeemer, we bow before you to honor you for bearing our iniquities and suffering separation from the Father because of our sins. Master, we rejoice that you conquered death and are alive forevermore for us, advocating for us in our weakness and failures, strengthening us by your Spirit, loving us always in all circumstances until you return for us and we bow before you, our Lord and our God. Even so come, Lord Jesus!"

Adoration of Christ for the Cross

Sin is past, your blood now cleansing.
Sons and daughters, one day reigning.
Crowns we cast, bowed down before you,
Shouts and songs lift up, adore you.

Adoration for creation!
Adoration for salvation!
Priests and Kings, without exception,
You for us achieved redemption.

Angels bow, with cherubs worship,
Creatures shout, with holy purpose,
All redeemed, all nations present,
"Worthy! Worthy!" voices reverent.

Adoration for creation!
Adoration for salvation!
Priests and Kings, without exception,
You for us achieved redemption.

Riches, glory, praise we shower,
For your mighty, awesome power.
Blessing, honor, wisdom proffer
For your worth, our lips do offer.

Adoration for creation!
Adoration for salvation!
Priests and Kings, without exception,
You for us achieved redemption!

Praying, praising, all now sing it
To the Father, Son, and Spirit.
One day then we'll see so clearly,
Finally then, He'll hold us dearly.

Adoration for creation!
Adoration for salvation!
Priests and Kings, without exception,
You for us achieved redemption!

SJH

Scripture Index